About the Author

Christie Goodwin is a visual storyteller passionate about
capturing the essence of live performances. She has travelled
the world, photographing everyone from Taylor Swift to Ed
Sheeran, Celine Dion to Jeff Beck, Camila Cabello to Nick
Cave, Status Quo to AC/DC. Her images have graced the pages
of some of the world's most prestigious publications. When she
is not behind the lens, she can often be found mentoring
aspiring photographers or working on a photo book project. She
is also the mother of two adult children and loves spending any
free time with them.

Truth Be Told

Christie Goodwin

Truth Be Told

Olympia Publishers
London

www.olympiapublishers.com
OLYMPIA PAPERBACK EDITION

A CIP catalogue record for this title is
available from the British Library.

ISBN: 978-1-83543-003-3

The information in this book has been compiled by way of general
guidance only. Neither the author nor the publisher shall be liable or
responsible for any loss or damage allegedly arising from any
information or suggestion in this book.

First Published in 2024

Olympia Publishers
Tallis House
2 Tallis Street
London
EC4Y 0AB

Printed in Great Britain

Dedication

I dedicate this book to my daughter, Robbin. We did it!

Chapter One – How I Became Morbidly Obese

Above All, Avoid Falsehood, Every Kind of Falsehood,
Especially Falseness to Yourself – Fyodor Dostoevsky.

It's a cold Saturday morning in September and despite the sun peeking through at prolonged intervals, it feels gloomy outside. I've placed myself behind my little makeshift desk and fired up my trusted laptop to write my story. My story is a story that I never imagined I would be writing in a million years. It's a story about learning, growing, discovering and achieving something I never thought possible. This recounts my journey from where I was miserable about my weight and how I turned my life around. If you too feel as if your weight has taken you hostage, I invite you to read my story and I hope it can help you.

Let's get one thing straight from the get-go: my purpose in writing this book is as simple as a cup of plain yoghurt. I'm here to share my personal journey with weight loss, not to critique or cast judgments on anyone else's weight or path. By laying out my own experiences, I hope to offer a hand of support, maybe, a dash of inspiration or a chuckle, to those who find themselves on a similar journey. So, consider this book your judgment-free zone, where we're all in this together, striving for healthier and happier lives, one page at a time.

Like any good old story, this story has a beginning, a middle and an end. The ending of my story is mind-blowing, and I am so excited to divulge the conclusion of my story with you straight away. So, I have decided to start this book by telling you the ending immediately because this book warrants beginning on a positive note. Let there be no secrets between us. I am lifting the veil of mystery from the first chapter onwards.

Brace yourself because it's quite the ride! Here we go. I shed a whopping 60 kgs in just shy of two years. Go ahead, read that sentence again and let it sink in. It still feels a bit surreal, even as I write it down. It's almost like I'm describing someone else's journey, not mine. You know those stories you come across in magazines or hear from friends that leave you with a mix of awe and envy, thinking, "I could never do that?" Well, that's exactly how it feels like. It is as if it is someone else's tale, not mine. At least, that's what I am thinking now as I type down these words. But here's the twist, I've got to pinch myself and remember that this incredible journey is no longer someone else's story; it's mine! Yes, you read that right. It happened to me!

It's not just because I was uber excited to tell you the ending of the story I shared with you; I have an ulterior motive for doing so which will become more apparent in the second chapter.

Isn't it extraordinary how easy it is to see the beginning of things, but we can never quite see how it will end? Try this exercise for yourself and remember how often you have started something. When you start something, you tend to plan everything out, and your determination is on full blast. Your intentions are there; you have a clear view of the road ahead. You probably will have written down schedules and maybe even bought yourself some tools to make the whole journey easier on yourself. You got yourself a new journal and pen and may have planned things step by step. Your beginning is fresh and crystal clear, but you have no idea what the ending will look like. The end is still up for debate as you are unsure how far your determination will take; you cannot see beyond the well-planned first weeks with your new journal and pen. The reality is that we don't always get to know the ending.

I was all prepped and ready to roll. I got myself a journal and a shiny new pen, downloaded some useful apps, and stacked up on audiobooks. My game plan was set, but let's be real. My dreams weren't etched in stone. I allowed myself some wiggle room to tweak things as I went along. I didn't have the whole journey mapped out, but I sure knew where the starting line was. Today, as I am standing on the other side of the journey and let me tell you, never in a million years did I think that I of all people, would have been able to change my life, my health and my way of living in such a unique, life-altering way. If you are reading this and feel detached from losing a significant amount of weight, that is okay. I was there where you are now. I, too, would read stories about other people achieving their goals, and I would always feel detached from those stories. Trust me; I know what you are feeling and empathise with you. I'm sharing my story because if I can help even just one person, writing this book will be well worth it.

People who have known me since I was at my heaviest are always keen to learn how I lost all that weight. People never tend to ask you how you have gained weight, though; it's as if that secret was already out of the bag, but boy, are they eager to learn the secret behind your weight loss. They expect me to enlighten them with some innovative miracle diet which magically allowed me to lose weight. Here's the secret, there are no miracle diets and I don't have a clean-cut explanation for my weight loss for all to apply. Instead, it's been a journey of researching and reading till my brain felt like it was about to explode. It's been a journey of learning, growing, discovering, failing and getting back up again. But most of all, it's been a massive wake-up call realising that I have lied to myself for thirty years and purposely and knowingly had misled and deceived myself. Cue to the title of my book: *Truth Had to Be Told*. It's a story of all the stories that I told myself to avoid reality.

Let me take you to where it all began for me. Ever since I was a young girl, I have struggled with hypotension. I remember that I often felt quite tired and weak as a child. I needed eight hours of sleep; otherwise, I would walk through the day as if my head were in a fog. I always needed to eat breakfast; I would be wobbly all day if I didn't. It was just the way things were for me. Doctors reassured me that even though my blood pressure was always a bit on the low side, there were no real worrying issues with my health. All I had to do was adjust my lifestyle accordingly. I was never overweight or skinny; I was just your average child. Hypotension was a constant in my life; I learned to live with it over the years. I got frequent hypotension headaches, and there were many moments when I felt fragile, but then I would slow down for a minute, and things would always fall back into place eventually. It never got to such a point that I couldn't function normally.

That all changed when my daughter was born back in 1993. My pregnancy had been without any hiccups, and the delivery had been without any problems, but as soon as I came home with my new born baby, things turned around drastically. I felt utterly low, continuously without energy, and my headaches became constant. My head was in this ever-present fog which meant that I couldn't think properly, and I found it challenging to find my words or make sentences. I did recognise the feeling I had been living with my whole life, but this time, it manifested itself more

12

significantly. My usual go-to remedies to slow down didn't do the trick any more.

I struggled that first month at home and doubted whether this was just the hypotension messing with me. My mother-in-law eventually encouraged me to go and see my doctor as she thought I might be suffering from postnatal depression. I remember thinking that I was not feeling hopeless, or even unable to imagine being happy again, which is usually what depression feels like. But then I immediately doubted myself because maybe I didn't have the strength to handle hopelessness.

My doctor knew my history of hypotension, so he immediately took my blood pressure and sighed audibly. My blood pressure had dropped much lower than its usual low digits, and his diagnosis was simple; my hypotension was slightly out of whack. But as my blood pressure wasn't considered dangerously low, I shouldn't be too worried, and he sent me home with the advice to sleep as much as possible, eat good food and have a glass of red wine in the evening, he added as he closed the door after me. I found myself back on the sidewalk packed with the advice to eat loads, drink red wine and all would be well.

But all was not well because it gradually got much worse. I started to get these little blackouts randomly which had never happened to me before. I would sit in my chair feeding my baby, and while I gently turned my head, suddenly, everything would turn black for a split second. It scared the living daylight out of me. I became almost neurotically careful about moving around the house because I would never know when my next blackout would happen.

Hypotension is considered much less dangerous than hypertension as it can cause severe health issues but let me tell you when you suffer from hypotension, it is no walk in the park.

It rips the engine out of you and your life; you are left with a shell of your former self. You feel lifeless, can't think properly, struggle to form sentences, and are battling continuous headaches. The doctor once accurately described that a simple task like watching the TV while reading a magazine has become impossible, which was spot on.

I desperately wanted to feel better again, I desperately wanted to enjoy spending time with my new born baby and I desperately wanted my life back. No copious amounts of sleeping, food or bottles of red wine seemed to do me any good. Instead, I had become a lifeless blob. I had learned over the following weeks that once I started feeling dizzy, my hands became clammy and I would feel a pressure just above my nose that I was about to drop into a blackout. It was such an impossible situation, and all I wanted was to get off this merry-go-round, so I started experimenting to find a solution. For the following weeks, my kitchen was transformed into a scientific lab, and every day I would try to brew a new potion to find the ultimate cure. I drank litres of spinach juice and created revolting potions mixed with iron tablets by the gallon. You name your choice's fruit and vegetable combination, and I can confidently say I tried it.

A significant turning point was when I accidentally added too much sugar into one of my potions. That sugar intake had given me a small window of normality, and I knew I was on to something there. That is when I started regularly eating a spoonful of pure white sugar, which magically would make me feel almost normal again, albeit for very short periods.

This is how I started to manage my life, one sugar rush at a time. To be able to go to the shop, I would throw back two cups of granulated sugar, and I would be good as gold. As soon as I returned home, I would be lifeless again, but at least these quick fixes helped me return to normality.

One day though, things didn't quite go as I had planned. I had taken my quick fix of sugar and whizzed off to the shops, but somewhere in between, I had either been overzealous, or my windows of normality were starting to wear off faster. As I was patiently waiting in line at the tills, I sensed that I was getting lightheaded, my hands felt clammy, and there it was, the pressure above my nose appeared. I panicked as I knew what was about to happen, and for this split second, I thought of putting myself flat on the floor so I could safely sit out my blackout, but of course, my pride overruled that. I remained upright, clinging to my shopping cart as if my life depended on it. My lights went out, and all I could hear was the sound of the shopping trolley smashing onto the floor. The next thing I remember was lying in an ambulance and being hauled off to the hospital.

At the hospital, they rolled me into the A&E and the doctor tending to me seemed to take my situation very seriously. A series of tests and tubes followed, and twenty-four hours later, I was released from the hospital. I was prescribed a medication that would stop my blood pressure from flatlining, and because they couldn't find the origin of my problem, they told me that I might be taking the medication for the rest of my life. The doctor warned me that a side effect of the drug was weight gain, but after a while that would balance itself out.

And here's the thing, I wasn't concerned about weight gain. If you had told me there and then I would gain a hundred kilos but get my life back, I would have signed up without hesitation. All I wanted was to be able to function as an average person again, and that is precisely what the medication I was prescribed did; it gave back my life.

I took my medication religiously; I functioned like a normal human being again and gained about 13 kgs that first year. Everything was honky dory, but was it though? What I failed to recognise at that time was a residue of fear that had accumulated during my blackouts and the fainting incident in the shop, which I wasn't consciously aware of. Just the slightest feeling of faintness would send me into a tailspin of panic, and that is when I started to top up my medication with extra sugar intake. I convinced myself I needed those sugar rushes to prevent history from repeating itself. I consciously supplemented my medication with copious amounts of white granulated sugar. There you go; that is the naked truth. Infused by irrational fear, I lied into dosing myself numb with sugar. It was the first of the many lies I told myself.

Fast forward ten years, I had been taking my hypotension medication while simultaneously being on a sugar rave. I had arrived on the doorstep of obesity, gained about 35 kgs, give or take and seamlessly transitioned from what is considered a healthy weight to obesity. I wasn't happy about the weight gain; it sometimes worried me. Typically, before summer, I would start an extreme diet hoping that all the weight gain would magically disappear. I must emphasise 'magically', as that was always my aim. It shouldn't take too much effort; it shouldn't deprive me of my sugar raves because I had thoroughly convinced myself I still needed the sugar rushes to function normally. So, 'magically' was the only way I could lose weight.

Ooh, the glorious diets I sped through; there's a whole plethora of them and yes, I have tried most of them. There are the crash diets that magazines proclaim will get us thin in the blink of an eye. Well, those have been proven to be a bag of nonsense because I never shed a pound. There are the liquid diets, the food-specific diets, the low carbohydrate diets, the detox diets, and the fasting diets; there are so many diets, promises, choices, and so many letdowns. Then there were the diet pills and supplements that promise us to lose weight while we sleep all by themselves. Again, they don't work, at least not for me.

At some point, I saw a doctor who claimed to have some miracle potion. I went to see this doctor every week like clockwork. He administered a clear liquid concoction with a syringe in my upper thigh every visit. That was it. One shot, no diets, no exercise, just one shot, and I lost weight. In all fairness, he was on to something there, as I did lose about 3 kgs in a month without dieting, without having to skip my sugar binges. Then into the third month of treatment, I started getting heart palpations, and it felt as if I was about to have a heart attack, so I didn't go back to him. That was the end of that success story.

I had convinced myself that the main reason for my weight gain was my medication, not my sugar raves. It's funny looking back at it now, but it didn't even cross my mind that taking in sugar as I did was causing my obesity. Because the medication was the culprit in my deluded mind, I decided to break up with my long-trusted hypotension medication. It was a decision encouraged by some practical reasons as well as I had changed GP and didn't want to go through the whole process of being tested again, so I chose the easy way out. I signed up with my new GP, didn't mention my history of hypotension, and went cold turkey while expecting immediate weight loss. The opposite happened, as you can imagine. The headaches almost immediately returned, and the dizzy feeling returned, so I substituted my medication with even more sugar rushes.

My standard 'go-to remedy' for the years that followed was one can of sugar-filled soda and a full bar of milk chocolate which always put me straight back on my feet. Of course, this sugar rave would always fix my problem for a hot minute so that I would revert to them multiple times a day. I'm not going to lie, I did struggle quite a bit, and the hypotension remained my constant companion. Still, I had a somewhat regular life by eating copiously, topping up with sugar by the gallon and my 'Soda & Chocolate' quick fixes. I never went out without a can of soda and a bar of chocolate. At work, I had a drawer filled with soda and chocolate. Next to my bed, there was always a can of soda and a bar of chocolate. I was never going to let my hypotension rule my life again. Instead, I let soda and chocolate take over the wheel. Of course, my ingenious self-help system also meant that I kept gaining weight.

Eventually, the day arrived when the scale had finally tipped over 100 kgs. I reached the point of 35 kgs over a healthy weight. I find it challenging to convey the profound significance of that minuscule shift, from 99.9 to the large wholesome hundred. Nobody ever tells us about this or warns us of its effect on us, but a change happens. In my mind, the needle went from; everything is still possible to all is lost; it went from I am a human being to a disgusting creature. It is never spoken about because once we are at that point, we hide in shame; we will not tell anyone what is happening to us and how we feel about it. At least, that is what it felt like for me. So, if you are reading this and your scale still shows that you are not over that 100 kg weight barrier and can relate to my truth so far, I encourage you to keep reading, as this could help you. It's an internal mind switch. I ULTIMATELY GAVE UP ON MYSELF once I went over the hundred Mark. I was obese, and there was no more coming back from it. I had crossed the point of no return.

One aspect of my journey that had been concealed from me

was the transformation of my personality in tandem with my changing weight. Unbeknownst to me, I underwent a gradual and subtle metamorphosis, becoming an entirely different individual. In hindsight, I can now discern how I instinctively adapted my behaviour to align with my shifting physique. It wasn't just a matter of outward appearance; my cognitive processes underwent a profound rewiring. Among the facets of my personality that underwent alteration, one noticeable change was my inclination towards withdrawal. I no longer sought attention, striving to blend into the background skillfully. The vibrant, outgoing person I once embodied had transformed into a reserved observer during the peak of my obesity. My self-esteem dwindled in parallel with the weight gain, and my conduct followed suit. When faced with dissenting opinions in conversations, I found myself more inclined to agree rather than assert my own viewpoint, as I harboured doubts about being taken seriously. Seeking assistance or guidance from others became daunting, as I wished to avoid drawing any unnecessary attention. My entire thought process had conformed to the contours of my overweight body and the diminished value, I assigned to it.

I also became increasingly lazy. I'm not naturally lazy, but I soon became crafty in avoiding strenuous exercise. For example, I would rather sit on a bus for an hour instead of taking a fifteen minute tube ride to a particular destination if I could avoid climbing those torturous stairs awaiting me at the end of the tube ride. Climbing stairs was the worst because it would leave me breathless after the fourth or fifth step, and I couldn't allow anyone to notice how breathless that made me. It would become this whole struggle of pretending and keeping up appearances. When I finally reached the top of the stairs, it felt as if my lungs were ripping my body apart.

Sometimes, I'd catch myself in a bit of a negotiation dance. It wasn't a fancy business deal, but rather me trying to work out the best way to skip out on walking. Yep, I had a knack for creating creative excuses to dodge any exercise. Every day felt like a bit of a tightrope act, balancing the needs of my overweight body and the strain it sometimes put on me. It wasn't just about choosing comfy seating or avoiding certain activities; it was about constantly adapting to my body's unique demands at that time.

Then there is the delicate subject of clothing sizes that I must also talk about. I had gone from a UK size twelve to a UK size twenty-four. I shall not mince my words here because that would not be truthful, but even though we know the truth of our size, we don't want the world to know it, so we hide it. Somewhere in my deluded mind, I thought that I was the only one who knew this truth and that I got away with it. At the height of my obesity, I was wearing shapeless, oversized clothing, which in my mind, hid my body perfectly and no one would notice how big I was. I truly believed that. Unsurprisingly, I could no longer shop at the high street boutiques, but instead, I got my oversized shapeless clothes from specialised shops.

My daughter, who loves to go shopping, would often ask me to accompany her to her favourite boutiques and I would break out in a sweat just thinking about the ordeal that awaited me. No matter how hard I tried to pretend, I couldn't help but feel like an elephant trying to squeeze into a delicate teacup when entering. Those boutiques seemed to shrink as soon as I walked through the door. I could practically sense the store attendants' curious glances and unspoken judgments. I could almost hear them thinking, "Why is she even in here?" as I awkwardly sifted through clothing racks. It was like a spotlight of self-doubt shining down on me while I was constantly battling between wanting to be there for my daughter and the overwhelming feeling of not belonging.

As time passed, a sense of dread began to creep in whenever I had to shop for plus-sized clothing. It was like I had built this mental ledge of embarrassment, standing on the edge, peering down into a pit of self-consciousness. With each shopping trip, I anxiously anticipated the moment that even a size twenty-four wouldn't fit me. Walking into those plus-sized stores felt like entering a realm of uncomfortable inevitability. The familiar dread would settle in as I browsed through racks of clothing, my mind echoing with doubts and fears about my size. I had become my worst critic, imagining a future where even the largest sizes couldn't accommodate me. It was like a looming shadow of self-doubt that cast a dark cloud over what should have been a simple shopping experience.

Eating in public was another torment for me as I would feel continuously judged. It wasn't just in public, but I felt judged whenever I was around food. Although, to be fair most of the judging took place inside my head. I used to feel as if everyone was staring at me and convinced myself they were thinking: "Look at that big woman stuffing her face." I used to binge out of sight of others to avoid judgment from others. Out of sight, out of mind, right? Eating four sugar-glazed doughnuts somewhere in a back alley was acceptable to me. Eating one sugar-glazed doughnut in public was embarrassing. I couldn't see how I used to lie to myself at the time.

Part of me pretended to be okay with my weight, but another part would continuously judge and condemn me for being overweight. It was a constant duality that was going on inside of me, but what is the alternative? I was trapped in this obese body and did not see a way out.

I was convinced diets didn't work for me, and exercising? Give me a break! I didn't have the energy to exercise, and let's face it, I would look too hideous even trying it. So basically, I had become a prisoner inside my overweight body and had to accept my faith.

Let's delve into a candid moment here. Deep down, I carried a weighty concern about my weight, even though I'd never openly admit it. It wasn't about vanity or appearances; it was about my health, something I took seriously. I was acutely aware that my excess weight could potentially harm my body.

This silent worry was like a constant companion, quietly urging me to pay attention to the potential consequences. I knew all too well that carrying excess kgs could put a tremendous strain on my health, from increasing the risk of chronic conditions to impacting my overall well-being. It was a delicate balance of acknowledging the issue without voicing it aloud as if saying it out loud might make it even more real.

Then menopause knocked on my door. Menopause usually causes disruptive symptoms, but, in my case, it didn't affect me in the slightest. On the contrary, I felt much better than I ever had done before. I didn't quite register it initially, but I realised I hadn't had my typical hypotension headaches over time. Somehow, I didn't need to revert to my quick fixes. Let's not kid each other here; I was still going strong on my sugar rushes, but when occasionally I missed a sugar intake, nothing happened, no dizziness, no headaches and no weaknesses. My suspicion was confirmed during a routine GP visit when the doctor told me my blood pressure was normal. That was a sentence I had never heard before, blood pressure normal? I couldn't believe what I had heard. I still vividly remember asking the doctor to retake my blood pressure to make sure, and he confirmed after the second 'pump and release' that my blood pressure was perfectly normal.

I tried to make sense of this, what had happened. Did this mean that I was finally cured? I had mixed emotions as, from one side, I found the news quite unbelievable and then again, how brilliant was it that my dark ghost who had walked alongside me for most of my life, interrupting my life at its own will, had finally left me for good? It almost sounded too good to be true, so I kept it my little secret and did not share it with my family. Just in case, the dark ghost had just taken a little holiday and was planning on returning to its usual position. Here I was, walking back home, most likely cured of a lifelong condition that had weighed so heavy on me for most of my life, and all I was left with was a scale that almost reached the maximum digits it provided. I did play with the idea of going on a diet in the weeks after the revelation. Still, I immediately discouraged myself from doing so because the enormous amount of weight I had to lose seemed unattainable. I assumed that unless I had one of those invasive surgeries where they sealed my stomach, it would be humanly impossible to lose 60 kgs by dieting. Having the surgery wasn't an option either that I was willing to undertake because of the invasive nature of it. So, I left it at that. To this day, I remain unsure if I would have succeeded if I had started a diet at that point. I doubt it.

Chapter Two – Climbing a Mountain of Information

"Pursue Knowledge as Though It is Your Lifeblood, Then You Will Know Greatness" – Monique Rockliffe.

A global pandemic put the whole world on a gigantic pause. The government set a lockdown in place, which they initially suggested would last only a couple of weeks but became one of the longest and strictest lockdowns the world had ever seen. By April 2020, 3.9 billion people were in some version of lockdown.

Because of the lockdown, I couldn't work, so the first few weeks, I found it quite exciting, albeit restrictive. I found myself with an abundance of free time which felt like a luxury because I had time to catch up on all the Netflix shows I had wanted to see and read the books I had been putting off, and of course, I did much eating as well.

Those first few weeks, I went through all the things I had been putting off until boredom kicked in, which I filled up with eating and snacking and then some more eating and then some more snacking. I suddenly found myself desperately searching for something new to keep me occupied while I was okay with doing nothing; I always liked to have my brain challenged. That's when I opened the gates to the universe of audiobooks and podcasts, which took me on a wild rollercoaster ride. I chose to listen rather than read because that would leave me room to do other things, like housework.

At first, I didn't pick and choose but randomly listened to the first audiobook in the suggestions. I covered a broad spectrum of topics from art history to quantum physics, negotiating in a hijack situation, and creating a perfect Feng Shui balance in your home.

One fateful day, as if by cosmic alignment, I stumbled upon a podcast featuring none other than Ricky Gervais as a guest. Little did I know, this serendipitous encounter would ignite the first flicker of a profound realisation within me. Amid the episode's banter, Ricky casually divulged his secret to managing his weight – a quirky ritual involving an exercise bike and a tempting block of cheese, his undeniable weakness. The simplicity of his approach struck a chord, almost as if it were a goal within reach for anyone. That single sentence etched itself into my consciousness, sparking an insatiable curiosity. No longer content with the one-size-fits-all advice from mainstream media, I embarked on a journey of self-discovery, determined to unravel the mysteries of my own body and its relationship with weight.

And so, at this point, I embarked on an exhilarating ascent up a towering mountain of knowledge, a journey that would prove to be both daunting and immensely rewarding. I opened myself up to a world of information that is vast and unfathomable! My exploration led me to delve deep into the intricate workings of the human body's energy dynamics. Every action, from the subtlest movements of our heart and lungs to the operation of all our organs, is fuelled by the enigmatic force of energy.

As I ventured further, I unearthed the fascinating secrets of our metabolic rate – that intricate balance influenced by age, gender, and activity level, determining the body's insatiable hunger for energy. The veil lifted on the function of our metabolism itself, and the interplay of glucose and insulin. I taught myself how saturated fats wove into this intricate tapestry, and so I reshaped my understanding of nutritional goals and paved the way for a new path to wellness.

As I listened and took in all that information, my perception of dieting slowly started to shift. Take, for example a calorie. My mind had always translated a calorie to this malicious content of food which ultimately made me fat. But I got to see a calorie as merely a measuring tool to calculate the chemical potential energy for our body. For example, we walk into our local coffee shop for a coffee and a bagel. These days we can often find the calories marked next to the price on the counter. Let's say the bagel has 350 kcal. This means that this bagel has the potential to provide our body with that amount of energy. Although I was long aware that our body needs fuel to function, listening to these audiobooks gave me the clarity to change my perspective; calories are not why I became obese.

As my research continued, I stumbled upon another epiphany. It's not all about calories, saturated fats and glucose. Most importantly, it's about how our brain works, the relationship between our brain and food, the psychological patterns of eating, and where they stem from. So, there was much more to research, and my knowledge broadened daily as I climbed that figurative mountain.

I enjoyed the learning process because something new would leave me in awe every day, I would discover another little bit of information that would change my thinking. My lockdown days were filled with learning, researching, meditating and eating. When I look back at that period, it leaves me with a feeling of nostalgia. I am very aware that Covid and the subsequent lockdowns put an inconceivable strain on many people, but for me that period of having so much time on my hands was just what I needed. It allowed me the time and space to educate and re-educate myself.

It struck me that the knowledge I acquired should have been part of our fundamental education from a young age. It raises a thought-provoking question: why aren't essential lessons about our health and well-being prioritised in schools, instead of, say, delving into the conquests of Napoleon? This valuable information holds the potential to benefit everyone, guarding against the pitfalls of misinformation and equipping us with the tools to lead healthier lives.

In Europe, one in six adults are obese, and in the US, one in four are obese. Obesity is a severe health problem in our society, leaving me to wonder why we don't try to educate the next generation from day one so we can prevent many health problems in the future. Everything I learned in that period has been integral to the success story I write down today.

For example, we are advised to follow a diet when we gain weight. Unfortunately, the term diet has become such a lose-throwaway term connected to weight loss which is only partially accurate. A diet implies using a specific nutrition intake pattern for weight management but can also be for health management reasons. Someone who has diabetes, for example, will be required to follow a particular diet to maintain good health.

It's crucial to dispel the myth that diets are a magic wand for weight management. Contrary to popular belief, they aren't quick fixes, nor should they be treated as such. Diets come into their own when we've indulged a bit too much during holidays or celebrated with abandon after a festive season, and we're yearning to shed those extra kgs that have stealthily crept in.

They often serve as a short-term strategy for fine-tuning our nutrition to align with our weight goals.

But here's the catch: the misconception is that a diet can universally address any weight issue, and that's where the notion falters. If diets were truly the silver bullet solution, the global obesity epidemic wouldn't loom as it does today. It's a complex issue, and the belief that a mere diet can unravel it oversimplifies the whole process and blindly ignores the crucial factors contributing to our collective struggle with weight.

The mainstream media and the big advertising companies ride on that train and make us believe that quick fixes work to lure us into buying their products or their weight loss schemes. Let's not forget that the diet industry is a multibillion-dollar thriving business because of this.

Diets for weight management are focused on helping us externally; they are geared to the right side of the brain, the analytical side. The typical diet module never considers the left side of the brain, which controls our eating habits. I'm not saying that diets don't work because people lose weight following a strict diet and commit to every step. But as time passes, the left side takes over the steering wheel again, and often all that weight will come back on. Sounds familiar?

Something, I had never considered before I started this journey was people struggling with their weight because of a historical pattern. I read this article about a woman who used to binge tubes of chocolate syrup every day secretly in her pantry behind her kitchen. She explained that she couldn't help herself, but every morning after breakfast with her family, she would retreat to the pantry, dig up her secret stash of chocolate syrup and consume the contents of a tube in one go. In the article, she continued that she had tried and failed every diet under the horizon. Consciously she knew that drinking the chocolate syrup wasn't right, which is why she hid it from her family, but just like me, she lied to herself and convinced herself that if she had the tube concealed when nobody saw her eat it, it hadn't really happened. Many years later, she went into therapy, and that is where her therapist made her realise something she had long forgotten. As a child, she had been quite a fussy eater, and after a while, her mother discovered that chocolate-covered pancakes were the only thing she would actually eat in the morning. From that moment onwards, her mother made her chocolate-covered pancakes every morning because anything was better than not having anything in her stomach when she left for school. She also recalled that she continued eating her chocolate-covered pancakes every morning when she went to college. It was only when she moved in with a boyfriend, and he put boxes of cereal on the table for breakfast that she found herself struggling, and that's when she started her habit of eating chocolate syrup secretly after breakfast. For us reading this story, it seems obvious why she was gaining weight, but don't underestimate the brain's power. I, for one, totally understand how she deceived herself for so many years and told herself lies to survive.

For someone else, the reason might stem from their cultural surroundings. This is again something I didn't realise until I read about it, although I had encountered a clear example of it in my circle of friends. About twenty years ago, I had a friend who struggled with her weight, just like me. We would often sit in the breakroom complaining to each other about our weight. One summer evening, she invited me to her house for dinner with her family. I joined her large family around the table; it was a wholesome experience. The wine flowed copiously, and food was passed on large trays while the atmosphere was electric, filled with laughter and joy. Her grandmother walked around with a large serving tray, and before my plate was empty, she would refill it while encouraging me to eat well.

As I left her home that evening, I told her that I had loved my time with her family, and she chuckled. "It's like that every evening here." I didn't realise it back then, but now I see that her weight struggles stemmed from her cultural environment. We often see when grandparents, who probably have seen hardship, feel that life is at its best with abundant food and sharing it with their loved ones. I also think that's a hard one to break because I have experienced one evening with them, and it was a blast.

For some becoming obese might be a gradual pattern to mask or solve a problem or cover a trauma. One story I recall reading was about a man who had been verbally abused by his mother his whole childhood. Whenever he did something, good or bad, she would scold him, telling him he was ugly and worthless. She used to say to him he was the worst mistake she had ever made. As a child, when we are called these words by someone we look up to for guidance, those words become our truth. During his adolescence, he started binge eating, subconsciously wanting to match what he had been taught. He tried to reach the persona his mother had taught him he was. He aimed to become what society deemed ugly. It's not as if he sat down and said to himself, I'm going to stuff my face so I can be ugly, but instead, an invisible subconscious mechanism did that all for him. His main struggle was that he had to override the self-image he had before he could even consider losing weight and becoming healthy again.

That is the reality of obesity. Obesity doesn't occur because we occasionally consume too much food. Instead, it is a pattern of continuous abuse of our body, and we all have our reasons why. Whatever the reason, it is our starting point of this journey. As my daddy used to say, we cannot fix it if we don't know what is broken.

The important message I took away from this is that I understood that I had gradually abused my body, and I could not rely on dieting any more as it would defeat its purpose. The right side of my brain could handle a diet, but I understood now that my left side of the brain would eventually ruin it all for me again. Going forward, I needed to find my smoking gun, my reason why. Only when I knew the reason why I had abused my body like this would I be able to tackle the pattern of abuse that I had become so accustomed to.

As you have read my history, my smoking gun might be crystal clear to you, but it wasn't all that clear to me. The main reason why we often don't see things is because of all the lies we tell ourselves. I said to myself that the reason why I became obese was because of the hypotension medication I had been taking for almost twenty years of my life. Even when I eventually dropped the medicine and kept gaining weight, I would not divert from the story I told myself. It was the medication; it wasn't me. I am not ashamed to admit that it wasn't until a couple of weeks into listening to the audiobooks that my penny finally dropped. I had been oblivious to this fear that had taken over thirty years of my life. It wasn't the hypotension medication, but my obsessive sugar intake stemmed from this fear of fainting. As I write this down now, it sounds so trivial. Fear of fainting got me to this morbid obese state; to keep control over my body, I completely lost control of it. How absurd is that?

Whatever your reason and however deep-rooted it lays, you probably lost control while trying to keep in control.

Somewhere during all my research, the same word kept

popping up. Lifestyle change. A lifestyle change was required if I wanted to improve my health and change my body, as it would require more than just dropping a few meals and avoiding sugar. It would require a complete overhaul of my habitual patterns within my lifestyle. Binging sugar to control not fainting was a regular pattern that became part of my lifestyle.

Changing a lifestyle sounded so invasive, though; at least, that is what I thought when I first realised this was the way forward. I was used to doing things my way; I was comfortable with my life, apart from my weight. Changing my lifestyle sounded very disruptive to me. This is the moment that the truth must be told; it was a very confrontational moment I had with myself. I had to be honest and accept that my lifestyle, no matter how comfortable or used I was to it, it hadn't done me any favours. My lifestyle was arguably faulty, and I had to change it to improve my health and physical appearance.

Let's pause for a moment because this is a significant juncture in my journey, one that shouldn't be rushed over. Maybe you've noticed it too, that there's often a wide gap between knowing the facts and being truly ready to change. Some people may grasp this concept immediately, and if you're one of them, kudos to your unwavering determination. As for me, I needed more preparation to flip my lifestyle on its head; I was busy searching for excuses to avoid it.

It's crucial to be open about my resistance and its reasons because, honestly, many of us can relate. It's all part of a pattern we've danced to for a long time. My excuses were like this mental picture I'd painted, a stereotypical image of a woman who's a gym enthusiast who starts her day with yoghurts and fruit, nibbles on salads, and practically swims in water. Now, if it suits you, there's nothing wrong with that lifestyle, but it just didn't fit me.

I was this close to waving the white flag, ready to surrender to the familiar embrace of my old routine. I mean, why change a good thing, right? But then, like a plot twist in a blockbuster movie, I stumbled upon a tale that woke me up out of my rock-solid convictions.

The story goes as follows, once upon a time, in a quiet neighbourhood, there was a man who followed the same daily grind without a second thought. Every morning, he'd strut past a house, and there, sprawled out majestically on the porch, was a dog. This dog had a peculiar habit. It groaned as if in agony, all while lounging in what appeared to be the lap of luxury. Weird, right?

Now, here's where the narrative takes a wild turn. The man, unable to quell his curiosity, decided to channel his inner detective and confront the mystery head-on. One fine day, as he spotted the homeowner diligently tending to his garden, our intrepid traveller seized the moment.

Summoning his courage, he approached the fence and, with politeness, inquired, "Excuse me, sir, I've noticed something rather perplexing. Your dog, on your porch, is always groaning in apparent discomfort. Is there something amiss with your furry friend?"

And here's where the homeowner dropped the bombshell. With a sly grin, he replied, "Oh, that old thing? Well, you see, my dog likes to lounge on a nail sticking out of the porch floorboard. It's not the cosiest spot, but it grants him a front-row view of the world, all while basking in the cool shade. He's so used to it that he'd rather endure a little discomfort and groan about it than change his spot."

This tale struck me like a bolt of lightning. How often do we cling to our own 'nails', groaning about our routines and habits, all while there's a world of comfort and change waiting for us? It's a stark wake-up call that sometimes, we're just like that dog, wedded to our discomfort zones.

This story was a huge epiphany for me, a lightbulb moment so bright it could blind you! I suddenly had this mind-blowing revelation as I realised, I was like that stubborn dog resisting change! My trusty scale had been screaming 'morbidly obese' at me, but I brushed it off as mere numbers. Who needs numbers, right? They certainly didn't stop me from living my best life. I was as snug as a bug in a rug, doing everything I loved without a hitch, and not a single medical issue in sight. So why rock the boat? Why, I asked myself, would I even think about changing? I was cosy in my comfort zone, basking in the warm embrace of familiarity. And then, BAM! The revelation was an 'aha moment', I realised that because I wasn't uncomfortable enough, I resisted the idea of change like an old dog.

Remember when I told you in the first chapter that I had an ulterior motive for unveiling the ending of my story at the beginning of my book? I told you about my fascination with how we always see the beginning clearly but rarely see the end. I was comfortable lying on the nail and moaning about it; no matter what I started, I never saw the ending clearly, so I remained laying on the nail on that porch, just like the dog in the story.

There is a reason why you picked up this book, and I may not be a mind reader, but your motives extend way beyond finding a good book for a simple night's read or to entertain you on your next long-haul flight. The subject of this book is what draws your attention because you might be stuck somewhere in a pattern that hasn't served you well. You too maybe laying on the proverbial nail just like I was. Like me, you might have tried diets and implemented changes hoping that something would shift, but nothing quite stuck. I understand you. I was there, I too was comfortable with my lifestyle, and I too was used to the patterns I had created, so there was no urgency for change. But secretly, underneath all that bravura and pretending to be okay with who I was, I craved a change. I remember thinking how nice it would be if it were only possible to change, but since there was no immediate urgency, I dabbled on through the winding wild stream of life.

Because I understand you, I dangled a carrot before you in my first chapter. I told you that I lost a massive amount of weight immediately. Despite your comfortable situation, this enticing bit of information has made you pick up this book because it gave you hope and a feeling that maybe it was possible after all. I needed a carrot dangling in front of me, too, before I took lift off. Losing weight from where I was at that point didn't seem possible. I had long given up on myself in that department. I had convinced myself that the only way I could lose all my baggage was through an invasive surgery that I was unwilling to undertake because I had had a bad anaesthetic experience. I had no natural way out, so I gave up trying. Better even, I used to chime jokingly. "I don't do diets; they are against my religion."

It wasn't until I heard the Ricky Gervais podcast, particularly that one sentence where he described that he would jump on his exercise bicycle every time he ate a piece of cheese that I found my carrot dangling in front of me. Suddenly, it seemed attainable, and it gave me hope. So, I started my book by telling you the ending of my story so you, too, could feel that sense of hope because hope is reasonable and warranted. After all, I am living proof that it is possible.

Chapter Three – Breaking a Habit

"Chains of Habit are Too Light to be Felt Until They are Too Heavy to be Broken" – Warren Buffet.

Habits need their own proper chapter in this book because I have learned that not calories so much, but rather the good old habits were my true nemesis. The reason I became obese was that I ate too much, let's not beat around the bush about that. But the continuously unhealthy eating of sugar was purely based on a habit. Who knew? Right?

I understood that I had been lying to myself, so initially I thought I could turn things around by being honest instead, hoping that everything would fall into place that way. Well, let me tell you, it doesn't quite work that way. We can't underestimate the power of thirty years of lying to ourselves, coming up with every excuse in the book at every turn of the way. What baffled me the most was that it all happened smoothly and effortlessly, so much so that I wasn't aware of it until I pressed my nose against the facts. It's not like I ever thought about lying consciously. Somewhere internally, I had this trigger which set off whenever I would feel slightly tired or low on energy. This almighty trigger smoothly transitioned into me getting up and consuming an abusive amount of sugar. I wasn't aware of the motivation, so I didn't consciously act upon it. This left me to wonder what was it that instigated this action.

What was going on internally seemed confusing because it

was a spontaneous process beyond my awareness. It was time to face and understand what it was that thought consuming sugar would be a good idea. Somewhere in the realm of podcasts, someone mentioned that consuming food was our brain-controlled habitual pattern. Cue to my subsequent investigation, what is a habit.

Have you ever wondered where habits come from and why we have them? I must confess that I only really thought about habits after this journey. Habits to me were just habits; there are good and bad habits, and that's all there was to it in my mind. To understand habits, I delved into a whole new category of audiobooks and boy, was that an eye-opener!

When I first embarked on my research, I listened to the typical scientific podcasts explaining all the parts of the brain and their properties and mechanisms. Still, the more I listened, the less I understood because the brain is complex. Before I knew it, I had gone down this rabbit hole of brain-related podcasts, and the complexity of it was overwhelming, so much so that I began to question my sanity. I understood the basics of the brain's workings regarding consuming food, but it didn't apply to my situation. It was as if I was listening to stories about other people, but I couldn't resonate with them.

Through my rabbit hole free-fall, I stumbled upon the Huberman Lab Podcast. Andrew Huberman, PhD, is a neuroscientist and tenured Professor in the Department of Neurobiology at the Stanford University School of Medicine explores a wide range of topics relating to our mental and physical well-being in his podcasts. I found quite a few podcast episodes that touched on habits and eating. Andrew Huberman has a way of explaining things that feel relatable; however, he was talking with scientific names like the frontal lobe, the medulla, and the cerebral cortex; he always connects the scientific names to their functions, which makes it easier to apply to whatever you are looking for.

While listening to the Huberman Lab podcast, I translated those scientific names and their properties into objects I could identify with, and that did the trick for me. I just got it, like the puzzle pieces finally fell into place. So, in the future, I will tell you in my own words what I learned about habits and how they helped me turn things around in a big way. If you prefer to delve deeper into this subject, I encourage you to listen to the Huberman Lab Podcast, as Andrew Huberman has a way of explaining science eloquently.

Just picture this, a big old suitcase, which is a metaphor for my brain, which contains many objects but three of them are essential to our journey as they are the leading players in this maze.

One object is the analytical one which fires up as I plan to lose weight. I use the analytical one to organise my meal plans for the week, to set my goals, and to arrange whatever I need to execute my diet. This object thinks logically, and I use it consciously most of my waking days. This is also the part that tells me I shouldn't eat a bar of chocolate because I am on a diet. I like this one as it seems to be on my side and seems to understand what I want to achieve.

The second object is the emotional one. It's the part that gives me emotions from giddy happiness to crying my heart out to feeling over the moon and awful about my weight. It's also the part that gives me urges, fulfilment, desires and so on. I consider this one the naughty one because it gives me the urge to pick up that bar of chocolate in the first place. I can picture the tumult already in my suitcase when the analytical one says 'NO' to the chocolate, and the emotional one says go on and have it anyway, I urge you. I don't know about you, but I'm rooting for the analytical one to win.

The third object in my suitcase is the most trivial one I didn't know much about until I listened to the Huberman Lab podcast. It's the boss of both the analytical and the emotional one. The ruler, the emperor, the almighty one who knows and sees it all and never sleeps. It's the one that is always busy because it must ensure that everything works properly and that I function correctly. It controls all my involuntary survival instincts, like my body temperature, appetite, and reproductive instincts and monitors my basic physiological needs. Let's call this one 'the boss', and I will do so in the future.

From day one, the boss has been registering everything I do meticulously.

The boss operated 24/7 in survival mode right from when my heart started beating in my mother's womb. The boss takes up about ninety-five per cent of all the power inside my suitcase, immediately bringing things into perspective. I imagined the tumult between the analytical one and the emotional one. Still, that tumult has become insignificant now that I know the boss has an overpowering force in my suitcase. Because the boss has such a big job, he has a little helper. The little helper transforms the information he receives from the boss into what we call: 'a habit'. I suppose you could see it as putting a specific action on cruise control. Once the step is on cruise control, the boss supervises it to ensure it doesn't encounter any interference.

Habits may have a bit of a bad rep, but they are nothing to frown upon because even though we are not consciously aware of them, most practices are vital for our existence. Imagine habits as the well-worn paths your brain loves to tread. They're the behaviours you repeat without much thought, your brain saying, "Hey, this is familiar. Let's do it again!" Habits can be as simple as your morning routine, like brushing your teeth or brewing that first cup of joe. Or they can be more complex like hitting the gym regularly or scrolling through your social media feeds for hours. What sets habits apart is their automatic nature. You don't have to decide to do them consciously; they happen, like clockwork. Have you ever found yourself snacking while watching TV without even realising it? That's a habit in action! Now, here's the twist: Habits can be your best friend or your worst enemy. Good habits, like eating nutritious meals or studying regularly, can improve your life. On the flip side, bad habits, like smoking or excessive procrastination, can drag you down. Understanding how habits work is like holding the keys to your own behaviour. Whether you aim to build better habits or break free from the not-so-great ones, it all starts with knowing what makes those brain pathways tick.

The boss knows the essential functions for us to survive, but it also registers anything we do on a repetitive basis and tells his little helper to create it into a habit so everything can run smoothly. Most of our body works on repetition, breathing, sleeping, eating and walking, to name just a few.

For example, walking is such an important habit, and I never thought about it, but it's quite an undertaking when a baby takes its first steps. The baby will be wobbly on their feet, trying to find balance. It takes all their attention to make it to the other side of the room. Eventually, when the baby takes its steps repeatedly, the boss and its little helper create the function into a habit, and after that, we walk on cruise control. Just imagine that walking wasn't a habit. That would mean that you would have to learn to walk again every morning you wake up. Can you imagine that? I can't even picture what life would look like if we woke up early because we had to learn to walk again. That is why most of our functions in life are habitual processes, and most are very important to allow us to survive.

Take eating, for example; how odd it may sound, eating is a beneficial habit the boss created for us when we were mere babies to stay alive. A new born baby is fed about eight to twelve times every twenty-four hours during the first few weeks of their lives. The repetitive pattern is registered by the boss, who passes on the information to his helper, who creates eating into a habit. In the future, if you miss a feeding, the baby will receive the emotional impulses and urges for food and will cry in response to the impulses it feels. It alerts you that your baby needs feeding. The habit and the cravings are essential to maintaining the intake of calories that the body needs to keep all the organs functioning and to keep the baby alive.

Let's fast forward to adulthood; you, me, everyone, we all go through life pretty much on cruise control. Most things we do daily don't require much effort unless we learn something new or do something we are not used to. Whatever we know, as soon as we do it repetitively, the boss will pick up on it, and a habit is created.

So, what about bad habits, you may wonder? All habits are created when a function is regularly repeated. The boss is non-judgemental and doesn't put things in context; the boss doesn't know right from wrong, he only registers patterns, and when a particular way occurs, it will pass on to his little helper, who creates a habit so you can cruise control through life.

Let's say you are a smoker, which is considered a bad habit in our society today. It all began one day when you and your friends lit up your first cigarette after school on the corner of the park. From then on, you had a cigarette every day after school on that corner of the park. The boss registered that repetitive pattern and considered it vital to your survival, so a habit was created for you. Now, you are thirty years old, and you want to quit smoking. Well, that is a problem because the boss doesn't like any shift in patterns, so as soon as you interrupt a habit, it will jump into survival mode. The boss registered your repetitive smoking as a need to survive, so once you quit smoking, it will send out alarm signals to your emotional part, creating nice little urges to ensure you don't disrupt the habit.

However, although the habits are designed for survival, our free will makes any habit by merely doing something repetitive. The boss always operates in survival mode and will do everything in their power to ensure you don't disrupt habits. What is impressed on the survival part will be expressed.

At this point, I understood that eating is a habit, so how does this habit affect my weight loss? So, following that thinking pattern, I decided to drop sugar altogether from my daily intake. We all know I have been eating sugar repetitively whenever I was triggered for the past thirty years, so I understand now that the sugar rushes are most definitely registered in my suitcase as a habit.

For argument's sake, let's say I decided to kick my sugar intake habit on Monday morning. Monday by noon, I feel tired, and the trigger gets released, but I have decided not to act upon it and stay away from sugar; the boss registers the lack of sugar intake, and it nudges the emotional one to release urges and cravings for sugar with the intention that I will respond to the desire and thus survive. I'm not consciously aware of this process going on in my suitcase. Therefore, the urge wins over my analytical thinking as my primary human survival drive trumps logical thinking.

Once I understood how my suitcase worked and how habits were built into my daily routines, I thought I was doomed and ready to throw in the towel again. I couldn't envision how I would conquer those habits that were always switched on in survival mode. I feel now more than ever that it is essential that you realise that I did make it happen; I managed to lose all that weight despite the rock-solid habits and the internal survival fights between the boss, the emotional one and the analytical one in my suitcase.

My suitcase has been through the wringer, but I am on the other side now and here to tell you it is possible. Although I managed to get to the other side, my suitcase is still rumbling and I have a feeling it might be here for a while, I am unsure if it will ever go.

Just this morning, my survival habit reared up out of nowhere. I didn't sleep very well last night; I had been tossing and turning and had woken up regularly, and I woke up feeling deflated and low. I had an extra cup of coffee because I couldn't get going. It was one of those mornings; I'm sure you know what I mean. I placed myself behind my laptop and continued writing, and about two hours into the script, I went downstairs to get myself a drink. Then, without being conscious, I found myself in front of the cupboard, looking for a bar of chocolate. As soon as I had the bar of chocolate in my hand. I thought, *How did this happen?* I placed the bar back and turned around. I had moved throughout my morning in cruise control; the boss had registered me feeling low and had nudged my emotional part to engage the desire for chocolate. Luckily, as I went through this discovery process, my analytical function was switched on, and I questioned my actions. I reasoned that this bar of chocolate would relieve the low feeling, but only for a split second; it wouldn't last, and it wouldn't solve the fact that I had had a stormy night's sleep.

The bar of dairy milk chocolate weighs 45 g, so it looks like nothing much. Still, at the backside of the bar, it's printed that it contains 240 Kcal, which means if I consume the bar, I have the choice to either walk/exercise for an hour and a half or subtract any nutritious and fulfilling food worth of 240 Kcal that I was planning to eat that day. Then you and only you can decide if it is worth the quick rush of chocolate. Every day I encounter moments like this where I'm on cruise control and must recognise the urges now as they happen, or I'm off the deep end again.

We pretty much are on cruise control from the moment we wake up. Just do the exercise for yourself and picture a life without habits. You wake up, and you must consciously learn to walk again when you get your wobbly legs to the bathroom, where you must consciously think about how you will pick up your toothbrush, then figure out how to put the toothpaste on, then figure out how to brush your teeth, how to rinse your mouth. You will be wiped out from all the effort and concentration and probably be ready for bed again. Habits are necessary; moving through our morning on cruise control without too much conscious thinking is essential for survival.

Like the boss, I'm at a place now where I don't consider habits good or bad, habits are an integral part of our human process, but some habits should be reviewed and adjusted to our present situation.

The main thing to remember is that although it will not be easy, many people have successfully adjusted their habits. It begins with understanding our habits and our habitual patterns.

We need to know where they originate from, and occasionally, we need to switch off the cruise control and consciously respond to our urges. It would be best if we had a strong commitment that no matter what, we would conquer adjusting our habits. It would be best if I stayed sharp and focused at all times because the boss and my emotional one will try hard to prevent me from interrupting my habit.

That, in a nutshell, explains the habit process. Of course, let's not forget that the habit I created was a response to a trigger. If there were no triggers, there would be no habit. In my case, I get triggered when I feel faint, which I thought I could solve by consuming lots of sugar. What is interesting, though, is that it is scientifically proven that there is a five-second prelude to me losing control and throwing myself over to my urge. In that five-second moment, there is a mood shift caused. In my case, I feel faint, so my mood shifts from average to panic. If I could elevate my mood in that five-second moment, I would avoid the trigger, and the habit wouldn't be activated. In severe cases of obsessive-compulsive behaviour, doctors will try to elevate the patient's mood with deep brain stimulation, which results in the patient not falling into the obsessive pattern.

Although the control of the trigger seems out of our hands, we still have free will; we always have a choice. That is one of the most essential notions I have carried throughout my process. I always have the option of indulging or not indulging. Unfortunately, I cannot escape it, and the choice will forever be dangling in front of me. At any given time, I have the option, to indulge, and face the consequences of the indulging, which will lead me to a place where I wasn't feeling healthy and happy, or I choose not to submit, reason myself out of the habit, which takes effort and commitment to not give in to the urge. The choice is and always remains mine; I must assume control and own it. Unfortunately, because of the trigger and the habits, I cannot just jump on a diet and make everything better again; I can't rely on overriding a pattern for a short while; I need to commit to a lifestyle change.

It sounds simple as I write it down, but let's not forget that the boss doesn't like me interrupting my habit of eating sugar, so it fights back hard. Today I have come to a place where I can disassociate myself from the pattern. When I began this journey, the cries to continue my habits were deafening. I call them my noises. They are harmless; they are not real; they are just noises. I no longer need my survival one to protect me and the emotional one from seducing me with urges; my logical one knows as much. This doesn't mean knowing it made my habits disappear, but it's an important starting point. Daily I must make myself aware not to personalise my habits. They are NOT me; they might have helped me in the past, but they are not me. As a kid, I did not have a sweet tooth at all. My granddad used to challenge me that I would get my pudding only if I had eaten everything on my plate, which never deterred me. I didn't mind skipping my dessert if that meant I could leave the table early to continue to play. I can see now that consuming sugar is not part of my DNA.

When people can't kick a habit, they often tell themselves, see, I told you so, I am weak and I don't have the strength to change my practices, as if the habit is a part of who they are. This is untrue; your survival brain created your routine, and you can consciously change these habits. When you do that, you break your habits.

My lifestyle change included a diet, habit, mind-set, and an overhaul of my life so far. It sounds overwhelming, and I will not lie; it is. The biggest struggle for me was to let go of the lifestyle

46

I had maintained for the past thirty years because, besides the fact that I was obese, I was comfortable eating what I wanted and when I liked it and not having to count calories, never worried that I had to be continuously aware my habits, not having to be on continuous alert for my triggers.

We are creatures of habit, and change makes us uncomfortable; we don't like the effort and uncertainty of change. The first thing that popped into my mind when I thought about a lifestyle overhaul was what I had to give up. It never crossed my mind to think about all the things I would gain. That is what comfort does to us. When we are comfortable with something, and someone mentions the word 'change', we will first grab onto what we must give up. Why would we want to change our comfortable lifestyle and give up those things that made us happy? My main reason was that I wasn't comfortable with being morbidly obese, I wasn't convinced that I could change my health and weight with a lifestyle overhaul, but I was willing to give it a shot as I felt I was much better prepared now that I understood the workings of my suitcase. If there was any chance of me ever turning my life around, it was this moment.

The lockdown began in March, and by the time I had absorbed, processed, and understood all this new information, it was already September. I have complained about my weight for almost thirty years straight. How often haven't we said to ourselves, "I should lose weight", as if we suddenly make it all better by saying those words? Sometimes saying those words makes us feel a little better, as if we have relieved the stress of the burden weighing on us the problem with saying "I should lose weight" is the 'should'. See, the 'should' made me feel like my intention was there but less direct, less urgent. I know I must lose weight, and I should lose weight, but am I going to lose weight though? Big question mark.

It's a place I have roamed for so long and know very well. When making this statement, I often tell myself I'll start on Monday. What's with the 'starting on Monday' promise we make ourselves? Why is Monday better than right now in the moment? Again, I said it so often because it feels less urgent, it's like a delay of execution, and look, all that time that leaves us that we don't have to think about dieting and can still indulge in whatever we want. It's all lies we tell ourselves to ease our discomfort in the now.

Once I started facing all the lies, I had told myself in the past, I was left with only one way to go, being honest with myself. I committed to calling myself out when I was lying or trying to delude myself. From that day forward, I will never say 'I should lose weight' again because I know by saying that I am only fooling myself. I committed to becoming healthy instead.

A promise is like a bridge going from where we are to where we want to be, and on that gloomy Thursday morning in September 2020, I committed to be healthy from now on.

Chapter Four – Creating a Lifestyle

"The Way to Get Started is to Quit Talking and Begin Doing" – Walt Disney.

I got my ducks in a row, or so, I thought. Here I was I had listened to hundreds of podcasts and audiobooks and read a zillion of reports and articles, and now it was time to make that change in my life. Standing in front of the unknown seemed like a huge mountain to climb, and I will confess that although my intentions were filled with determination, my mind wasn't sure if I could ever see it through.

The evening before I was due to set off on my new path, I went through a grieving ritual; I kid you not. It was important to say goodbye to all the delights I had known and indulge once more. I treated it like the last meal you get on death row. The ritual included a copious dinner, of course. It was followed by not one but two desserts which I finished off with a packet of my favourite cookies. And to close it all off, I had one last regular Coke. Looking back at my actions back then, I realise now that my mind probably wasn't ready for it yet, and the whole grieving ritual was me desperately clinging to what I thought gave me the most pleasures in life. I honestly thought I would never eat cookies again, and I would never be able to drink a regular Coke again. I was terrified because I had no idea what to expect as I left my comfort food behind. It just felt very daunting.

Discovering that fear, at its core, is nothing more than a

collection of stories we tell ourselves has been a revelation. These stories, while often intimidating and seemingly impossible, are, in essence, the narratives we craft to safeguard our comfort zones. They're the scripts our minds recite to keep us cocooned in the familiar and the safe. Delving deeper into this understanding has allowed me to reframe fear not as an omnipotent force, but as a self-imposed set of tales waiting to be rewritten and challenged.

Your ideal lifestyle should be like a puzzle, where all pieces perfectly fit together, taking a full picture. The puzzle has five distinct chunks: Sleep, Hydration, Mind, Exercise and Food. When one of the puzzle pieces is out of sync, it will influence any or all the other puzzle pieces. Therefore, it is crucial to figure out a balance between the pieces, but more than that, we need to find a way to make the pieces fit to nicely to who we are and what we need.

Before we jump into the deep end, I will repeat this as it is essential, you need to find a way to make the pieces fit YOU! Although the media and advertising companies sell us the idea of perfect plans for all, trust me, no one plan fits all. A plan that includes all is a plan for failure. We have come this far, so we don't want to fail. The most important advice I can give you is that only you know what is feasible for you and what is not.

It would be best if you started by being completely honest with yourself, and whatever plan you set up, always make sure you remain true to yourself. If you build your plan and force yourself to incorporate pieces that don't fit you, then the likelihood of failure is guaranteed. Be honest to yourself and be true to yourself!

Puzzle piece one-Sleep. I never gave much thought to sleep; if I'm honest, it's just one of those things that you take as it comes. I planned to skip over this puzzle piece when I started this journey because I considered myself a good sleeper and never questioned how sleep affected me. Nevertheless, sleep is such an important puzzle piece. We are all very busy people and try to cramp as much as possible into our days. More often, we bite off chunks of our sleep time to do it all; I know I have. I have always been careless about sleep and never questioned how sleep affected me. Some days I wake up fit as a fiddle, and some days I wake up tired as hell, but I have always taken sleep as it comes. While re-educating myself, I had come to understand that sleep was a vital piece of the puzzle, and your sleep rhythm contributes to your overall well-being. Who knew?

Adults require an average of eight hours of sleep to regenerate their physical health, which we all know. I don't set a watch to monitor how much I sleep, but I do know that when I haven't slept well, I often crave food to pull myself through the day, so I figured that looking at my sleeping habits made sense.

I got myself one of those watches you wear while you sleep, registering your sleeping pattern. I already learned so much by reading the instructions with the watch. The leaflet explained that an adult should have between seven to nine hours of sleep, so that was an excellent goal to set up. The sleep rhythm gets divided into stages and logs time spent in each step of your sleep. There are four categories: awake, light, deep and REM sleep. First, there is the stage which is the time spent in bed before and after we fall asleep, but it also includes brief awakenings during our sleep. Light sleep is where our muscles relax, which is supposed to be the transition phase between our other sleep phases. Then there is the deep sleep which is the phase that focuses on restoring our body. Finally, there is the REM sleep which restores and re-energises our mind. The amount of each stage of sleep varies, of course, but as a good measure of an ideal night's sleep, we should go through four to five ninety-minute cycles that sample in different phases of sleep as the night progresses. Generally, each cycle moves sequentially through each stage of sleep: wake, light sleep, deep sleep, REM and repeat. Cycles earlier in the night tend to have more deep sleep, while later cycles have a higher proportion of REM. By the final cycle, our body may even skip deep sleep altogether. And did I mention that besides measuring my sleep cycles, I would wake up every morning to get an overall score of that night's sleep? That was the fun part, competitive as I am.

After that first week of wearing my sleeping watch, I opened the app on my phone to read my pattern, which was a serious eye-opener. As I said before, I thought I was a good sleeper. My sleeping pattern was all over the place, irregular and far from where it should be. My end score dangled between fifty-five per cent and sixty-two per cent, which could have been better. One of the main issues that stood out in my pattern was the amount of registered awake time. The graph looked like a Yo-Yo on crack bouncing up and down, and I wasn't even aware that I was awake so many times throughout the night. I knew I had to figure out why this was happening and how to change it.

I made little changes, one at a time, gave it a week, and revisited my scores to see if there had been an improvement. It is essential to take it step by step and make little changes in your habits to find out what works for you and what doesn't. For example, I used to have a warm drink every evening before I went to bed, and once I dropped my night-time drink, I discovered that I managed to fall straight into a deep sleep instead of yo-yo-ing in a light sleep wave.

Another problem that I never realised troubled my sleep is

that I suffer from Tinnitus. I always thought the sizzling sound in my ears was soothing, but one night and that was purely by accident, I fell asleep with an earbud playing soft music, and that night, I had such a steady regular sleeping pattern as I had never had before. So now I always sleep with soft music in my ears.

As my sleeping pattern gradually improved, I learned that I shouldn't drink anything at least two hours before bed; I have learned not to have any alcoholic drinks at least four hours before bed, which enables me to have long deep sleep periods. I have learned to watch something funny in the last half hour before going to bed; somehow, it has made it easier to fall asleep.

It has taken me some time trying and failing to find the perfect situation. Still, I found it a vast help wearing this watch to register my sleeping behaviour as it allowed me to see how the patterns evolved when I changed something in my routine. I have fine-tuned it over time and understand what works well for me. I still have nights I don't sleep enough and am still very restless, but they don't occur frequently. I mostly have good nights with regular solid sleep. I love it when my score shows eighty per cent or more. I once even scored ninety per cent, although that high score only happened once, it's like an elusive unicorn I got to catch once, but I know I will get there again. The cherry on top is that I learned that during deep sleep periods, I am burning off calories, so improving sleep has ultimately helped me with my weight loss.

Puzzle Two-Hydration. Hydrating ourselves is vital for our well-being despite not providing us with any food, but we all know that. Almost all our bodily mechanisms depend on water to function. Despite knowing all that, I have always struggled to drink enough. It has happened more often than I care to remember that I went hours without a single drop of liquid intake

53

because I just wasn't thirsty. So how much do we need to drink? The rule of thumb is that we lose about twelve cups of water through breathing, perspiring and urine and bowel movements, so we should at least take half of that daily. Anything above six cups is the way to go. Since we are on this path of breaking bad habits and replacing them with good habits, I have taken it upon myself to set a goal to take in at least eight cups of water a day.

Some days I succeed, and some days I fail. I started with drinking still water because that is what is recommended, but after my 3rd cup, I'd get nauseous, so I changed over to drinking sparkling water, and although the bubbles made it a little bit more pleasing, it still wasn't enough to keep me on track. I now have found that dropping a fruity cold-water infusion into my water bottle, which tastes nice, helps me keep myself on track and get eight cups daily. The cold-water infusion bags are like teabags; they are sugar-free, infusing your water with blended natural fruit flavours. This works for me, but as I said before, everything you do needs to be right for you. If you are anything like me and you struggle drinking water, let the fact that water flushes out fat motivate you. It sure inspired me to stay on track.

Puzzle Three-Mind. This was the hardest to conquer of all the challenges I faced. The funny thing is that once upon a time, I used to meditate daily to release stress and quiet my mind, but I had put it on the back burner while life took over. Somewhere along the way, my mind turned into my greatest enemy. Looking back on my old self, I recognise how stressed and anxious I would scurry through my days. Our mind is a powerful tool; no matter where we turn, we cannot escape it. I am fully aware of all that negative talking myself down I used to do. I was carrying a heavy burden of negativity, and there was no way I could change my life in that frame of mind.

First, I tackled the negativity that had lived rent-free in my head for too long. All that negative thinking significantly impacts how we feel mentally and physically. It was tough as I had fallen into this pattern of negativity which perfectly fitted my body. I had this evil little voice that had loyally condemned my appearance for years, and somehow I had to try to replace it with a loving, reassuring and, most importantly, cheerful voice! Of course, this couldn't just be reversed or turned off like a light switch. That's the moment I stumbled upon Gabby Bernstein, whose website is brimming with meditations and affirmations designed to empower you. Gabby has been a constant presence, guiding me through every stage, reshaping my pessimism with her spiritual wisdom, candid advice, and life-altering techniques that have completely transformed my journey.

Somewhere I had read, a psychologist referred to our mind as a glass of clear water, and over the years, we had scooped dirt into our glass of water, and now the water was all muddy. Our drink of water had become so cloudy and soiled that we could no longer see through it. If someone drops a coin into the glass of water, we wouldn't know because the water is just too mucky. It's physically impossible to scoop out the dirt because that would mean scooping out all the water, so the only solution available is to pour in clear fresh water until all the mud has rinsed itself out. That is exactly what positive reinforcement does to your mind. The more positive self-talk you have, the more positive the mind becomes. Be aware that if you are as deep as I was, it will be a slow process of two steps ahead and one step back daily, but as you go along, it does become more accessible. Be patient and kind to yourself. Today I am at a place where I still catch myself talking down on myself, but I know when that happens and will turn it around immediately. I deserve to be treated with respect and dignity, especially by myself.

It was time to find my inner balance once I had straightened out the negative self-image pattern. The positive in this mind transition is that taking care of our body naturally signals our brain that our overall stress levels can decrease.

If you were building a new home for yourself, you would have a blueprint that shows precisely how you want your home to look. You would wish the builders only to select the best wood and steel for building your home. You would like the best of everything. Consider your mind the new home you are making. Create a blueprint of what you want it to look like, then use only the best resources. You are building your mental home; your thoughts and imagery represent your blueprint. Hourly, moment by moment, you can create new positive thoughts, beliefs and habits you implement. This unique contemporary home is your personality, identity and life story. Don't settle for less; you deserve only the best.

You must create new habits that suit you. Focus on finding manageable practices that you can integrate into your daily routines. In the future, you can build on those routines as you continue reaching your long-term goals. One way I have is that every morning when I wake up, I think of a handful of things I am grateful for before I take my phone or have coffee. Usually, one of them is that I am thankful that I am about to drink a good coffee.

The contents of what we are grateful for are less important than the habit of pausing and thinking of things we can feel thankful for. This habit has helped me a lot in being less of a grump in the morning. Every morning, without fault, the first thing I do is say my gratitude.

Another habit I have put in place is meditation. Whenever I

feel overwhelmed, I stop, take three deep breaths, close my eyes and tune out. Even if it is only for a few minutes, I check out and let the world continue without me. At first, I struggled with this; I failed many times to keep this habit of relaxing my mind in place. Just don't give up on yourself; you've got this!

Puzzle Four-Exercise. I dreaded this part of the puzzle because the word exercise doesn't have a place in my vocabulary; it never had. I have never enjoyed any form of physical exercise, even as a kid; I dreaded PE and anything requiring physical strain. From the get-go, I feared that this was the part I probably would fail at. So, for all my people who loathe exercise in any shape or form, why don't we change the word 'exercise' into 'non-seated fun'?

My rational mind understood that having some 'non-seated fun' would be essential to my health as various podcasts I had listened to discussed how it affects our physical and mental health. However, my emotional brain had a 'twelve-volume hardcover – six-hundred-pages'-list of excuses ready not to have to commit to this. It wasn't just the fact that I loathe any form of exercise, but because of the size and weight of my body; it was just so hard to entertain the thought of doing anything remotely physical. In the end, the prophetic words of Ricky Gervais on his exercise bike still lingered in the back of my mind. So going by that little nugget of information, I bought myself one of these compact running machines to get my daily exercise sorted, hoping that in the secrecy of my own home, I would find the courage to start running. Here is the truth, though, we cannot adopt a lifestyle change that doesn't fit us. I cannot stress this enough, but finding something that suits you is crucial. It's a challenge because we are all different and have different interests, and often we are lured by exciting advertising to commit to something deep in our hearts that we know we won't see through. I knew I wasn't the running type when I bought the running machine, but I did it anyway. As you may have gathered by now, the running machine didn't last. I used it for a week and sold it the following week. Even though I had to find a way to stay active so my endorphins could help my brain and body function, running would never be the way.

The only thing I could entertain doing was walking. It sounds so ordinary, but everyone walks, even I walk. I was a master in trying to avoid walking if I could, but still, I sometimes had to walk to the shops and work; I guess I was a walker. I got myself one of those pedometers because if I were going to walk, I would not waste any steps at random but calculate them meticulously.

It was suggested left, centre and right that an adult walk at least ten-thousand steps daily. That first week wearing my brand-new pedometer proved another eye-opener as it showed that my daily step count didn't even reach thousand steps in one day. Instead of putting the bar too high and consequently failing, I set the pedometer with a goal of two-thousand steps daily. I had to do at least two-thousand steps in one day. I'll be frank with you; I failed that first month miserably and found myself shaking my wrist at the end of the day so it would register extra (fake) steps so that I wouldn't be too far under the two-thousand steps goal. I know, don't judge me, I lied to myself once again, but it was a real struggle to reach that two-thousand-step goal.

The moment I turned things around was when I didn't leave it to faith to reach the two-thousand steps goal, but I implemented a structure for myself. I decided to go on a daily lunch walk together with my daughter. At twelve, we would get ready and walk, or rather stroll, one circular route around the block.

Because I committed to her, finding excuses not to walk was harder. At first, those lunch walks were challenging, and by the time we had arrived at the top of our street again, I would take a second to lean against a wall to take a breather. The lunch walks made it so I reached my two-thousand steps goal almost daily. There was a transformation because if I hadn't reached the two-thousand steps, I would find myself stepping up and down my kitchen while cooking. Why waste time that you could fill up with steps?

After two months of lunch walks, I felt that walking became more manageable for me, and I didn't even need the stop at the top of the road any more. Somehow the regular pattern of walking had shifted my stamina. That is when we decided to add an extra walk around the block to the lunch walking route. At first, that extra street felt quite taxing, and I needed a breather at the top of the road again. Because of our regular lunch walks, I quickly reached my two-thousand steps goal, and most days, I even went over my goal. It did feel good when my pedometer sent me a message saying: 'overachiever'! A couple of months ago, I couldn't have imagined that ever happening when I shook the pedometer with my wrist to fake my step count.

That is when I boldly set my pedometer goal to four-thousand daily steps. The goals we set for ourselves are integral to our overall success in changing our lifestyle. It is essential, though, that we focus on setting realistic goals. Setting realistic goals that we can achieve and then building on them will help us maintain momentum and stay motivated.

At first, I felt I might have overdone it by setting my goal to four-thousand steps a day because that first month, I never reached my goal and almost lost the momentum I had going. I moaned about it to my daughter, and she suggested adding a morning walk to our daily schedule. I was hesitant initially, but I didn't want to disappoint her. Those first two months were tough. It wasn't so much walking because we still only walked around the block, and I had become used to that by now, but it was the regiment of having committed to doing it every day. I cannot tell you how many times I looked for excuses not to go for that morning walk, and I did cancel a few with some flimsy excuse, but seeing the disappointment on my daughter's face when I did that was just as tough. With the morning routine now incorporated, my pedometer had been sending me the 'overachiever' messages again, which made the suffering a bit lighter.

I wasn't anywhere near the ten-thousand steps a day yet, so I decided to up my personal goal to eight-thousand steps a day which seemed like a big step if you look where I had started from. Just like before, reaching the eight-thousand stages a day goal seemed near impossible, and what I had feared happened my daughter, suggested we'd incorporate an evening walk as well. While writing the process down, the timeline might not be clear, but I was almost eleven months down from where I had begun. In eleven months, I had gone from not reaching two-thousand steps a day to overachieving four-thousand steps a day and now, in the 11th month, I was pushing it up to eight-thousand steps a day.

It took an effort; I am not going to lie, it took commitment, but I wasn't pushing too far out of my comfort zone. It was just walking one step in front of the other at a leisurely pace but on a schedule, and the more I did it, the easier it got. I skipped several walks with silly excuses and almost always felt guilty as soon as I did it. I guess it's all part of the process.

The main takeaway is that we need to find something that

suits us. The non-seated fun must be something you can do without forcing yourself into something you cannot see through. Start small; remember, my first goal was two-thousand steps a day which was huge for me, but it was a goal I could reach. Find something that works for you and take baby steps into it.

It would be best if you had a schedule you could stick to because it is the only way to stay on track. I'm not too fond of schedules, but in the end, the programme helped me through it. You will find excuses to avoid your plan, and that is okay if you go back to your schedule the next day. Don't give up because you missed your schedule one day. There is always another day to get going again.

The most important one though is to have a motivator. For me, it was my daughter who kept me accountable and who helped me through it by joining me on my walks. You may have a friend or a family member you can count on to do this non-seated fun bit with. Maybe you have a dog that needs walking every day. Perhaps you have a new born that needs regular walking outside. Whatever it is, have a motivator to keep you on track. Whenever my daughter wasn't available, I would put my earphones in and listen to podcasts. I would plan it so that I knew I had to finish two podcasts before I could return home and I walked through them and got my steps.

Today my pedometer is set to the ten-thousand steps a day goal. I reached the goal that people should walk a day and trust me when I tell you that when I first started, I never dreamt this would be possible. I did it. I got there. Most days, I am over fifteen-thousand steps because I walk everywhere. I don't blink an eye at a three-hour walk. Guess what? I even own walking boots! Now that is a sentence; I never thought I'd hear myself say. I've come to a place where I thoroughly enjoy walking, and when there is a day that, for some reason, I can't walk, I feel yucky; I feel sluggish like a bear walking out of its winter sleep. To this day, I still find myself looking for excuses not to walk; I guess an old leopard doesn't change its stripes, but at least I am aware of it, and I know that I will feel better when I have done all my walking.

Puzzle Five-Food. Nutrition is an essential element of the puzzle. Usually, the one most weight loss programmes start with. I purposely saved it for last because I learned that if the first four puzzle pieces aren't in place, it doesn't matter what you eat; you will find it very hard to lose weight. Only when you have tackled the first four pieces are you ready to successfully tackle this one.

Eating within the measure of our body's needs is one of the most complex parts of changing your lifestyle. Grabbing a sandwich, eating a cookie, drinking a sugar-filled soda, or going out to dinner and getting your favourite pizza is easy. It's all part of what we are used to and what we have been doing up till now. This is our standard. Now, we must create a new normal that, in some cases, will be as far removed from our present ordinary as possible. It sounds daunting, but the daunting part is the stories we tell ourselves. If my usual were all that normal, my body would not be so out of the typical spectrum. Realising that eating healthy and within your calorie measures is not just about your weight is essential. It also provides more body energy, improves overall health, and increases productivity.

It is necessary to create realistic and attainable goals for yourself. I knew I ought to lose 60 kgs, but instead of setting that outrageous prominent figure as a goal, I put my plan to lose 5 kgs. Small goals and small victories are much more rewarding, especially if you have a long way to go, as I did. My logic was that if I could lose 5 kgs, maybe I would be ready to lose another

5 kgs after that. The small goals have been my way to success in whatever step I took in this process. It is essential that you can see the end goal.

It is also essential to allow yourself to enjoy food. It is not because you are changing your eating habits that food must be tasteless and boring. It is all about learning to balance and still enjoy the food you eat. From the start, I decided to allow myself to have one dessert daily. It is the first item I enter in my app daily. I have one dessert after dinner in the evening, no matter what.

As you go along, rewarding yourself when you have achieved a goal is also essential. When you have lost the first 5 kgs, treat yourself to something that makes you happy. It could be something small like a manicure, a new book or you can go and watch that film you want to see at the cinema. Be prepared for the fact that there will be times when you have a setback. You might have to go out for dinner with the family, there is a birthday party, or the office has organised a lunch. Don't let setbacks define your commitment. Setbacks happen; there is always the next day to get it right again. Don't let the setback be your excuse to abort.

I have found it best to plan my meals; I make a shopping list and figure out my calories before buying groceries. At the beginning of the week, I have already entered all my meals in my app, so I know exactly where I am day by day. I never buy premade meals any more as they are very high in calories; instead, I cook them as that will save me so many wasted calories.

And, of course, track your calorie intake, which is the most important one. It doesn't matter how you decide to track your food intake; find a system that works for you. Many apps are available and they all do the same thing. All that matters is that you must track everything that you eat. Everything! That will be an eye-opening moment for you as it was for me. Putting everything into the app means that when you clean vegetables and stick a carrot in your mouth while cooking, then enter the carrot into your daily intake. It sounds petty, but it makes a difference, trust me. It will require total honesty on your part. But don't worry; it is just between you and the app. You are the one who is accountable for doing it. If you don't lose weight, you cannot blame anyone but yourself.

Chapter Five – Commitment to Honesty

"Honesty is the First Chapter in the Book of Wisdom" –
Thomas Jefferson.

You might wonder what honesty has to do with losing weight but trust me; this chapter is an essential and integral part of becoming healthy in body and mind. Honesty seems trivial because we have been told to be honest and always tell the truth since we were kids. It looks so unambiguous to achieve. Being honest with ourselves now is a different story because nobody can make you accountable for what you tell yourself. We all tell ourselves stories sometimes. We might do it to explain overwhelming emotions, or we attempt to cover up authentic feelings that we may be too ashamed to let out. For some, it can be a habit that stems from childhood; for others, self-deception is an automatic process of attempting self-protection. We lie to ourselves to meet specific psychological needs that transpire. Sometimes it goes deeper than a conscious effort to avoid an uncomfortable situation. Sometimes it's an unconscious psychological defence mechanism that wants to protect us against scary or painful memories. So, in theory, we could say that self-deception is sometimes required to protect us. We may feel protected, but we should remain conscious that the feeling is an illusion we create through self-deception.

Sometimes this self-deceit becomes an obstacle when we slump into a deceiving pattern that becomes complacent. An excellent example is when we complain about something we feel unhappy about but then discard doing something about it. We, on purpose, deceive ourselves to cover up our true feelings. I have moaned for years that I wasn't happy about the size of my body and that I needed to lose weight, but at the same time, I genuinely didn't intend to take steps to lose weight actively. All I wanted to do at that moment was acknowledge forthrightly that I was aware of my weight problem, and I was aware that I had to do something about it. My moaning didn't serve me any purpose; it didn't help the problem; it merely subdued my conscience. I never realised the pattern I had slipped into, but I had another epiphany reading an article about body dysmorphia. Body dysmorphia is a severe condition, and even though I don't have body dysmorphia, the self-deception process that the patient applies in the report I read is strikingly recognisable. I identified that I was in an addictive pattern of self-deception. At the end of the article, the author challenges the reader with the question, "Has the story you have told yourself served you?" My answer to that was clearly 'no'. I leave a pause for you to answer that for yourself.

Being honest with yourself is much more complicated than it sounds. Being honest with yourself requires courage. It can sometimes be challenging to face the truth and even harder to act based on it. We tend to play these games with ourselves to minimise our feelings. We often convince ourselves of things that are not true so that we can feel better about our lesser ideal circumstances. We might convince ourselves that we have no control over our events while we always have power. It means that to be honest with ourselves, we must act and be courageous, which generally feels very scary. But honesty with ourselves is essential to our well-being and quality of life. Veritas Liberabit, the truth will set you free.

For thirty years, I had been deceiving and lying to myself, resulting in my becoming morbidly obese. Sure, my feelings might have been spared occasionally, but I had put my body through the wringer to spare my feelings. I dosed myself with a massive amount of sugar, but is that really what helped me, or was that just an illusion? Most likely, the medication I took kept me stable and going, and truth be told if my blood pressure had done another nosedive, I most likely would have fainted anyway. Luckily my fainting incident had been an isolated occurrence, so we will never know.

Still, my deception didn't protect me from anything when I look at the picture today. I lived under an illusion of protection from fainting, filling my mind with a coherent story about myself and taking in loads of sugar made sense to me in that story. While lying to myself was an act of self-preservation, living within that illusion severely impacted my reality. I faced the reality of my self-deception and recognised the toxic and unsatisfying habits I had created. I had felt stuck for so long, and that feeling had caused me so much shame and disappointment.

When I looked sincerely at my reality, I asked myself this question: what do I get not to see, not feel, not experience if I stay right here? Answering that question instantly revealed the invisible benefit of pulling myself out of my self-deception. It might be an interesting question to ask yourself. Write down your answer, and whenever you feel like giving up on yourself, return to the answer you have written down. I did that, and it has helped me through some rocky patches. I'm not throwing shade on this subject because, trust me, I know how it feels to be stuck in a self-deception cycle. I have been there and seen it and am wearing the T-shirt.

Be assured, that self-deception is a typical human practice. Especially in our society today, where we are under so much pressure, there is so much focus on how others perceive us. To get going, we must examine the deeper reasoning behind why we deceive ourselves so we can be ensured that it is not just a toxic habit that harms us more than it should. I don't take this topic lightly and understand that self-deception can be a survival tactic for people living in dangerous environments that they can't escape immediately. But I am taking a leap of faith here to say that if you have taken up this book from the bookshelf and went to the counter to purchase the book, you are ready to step out of the lie, which in itself is an act of self-preservation.

As soon as I had yanked myself out of my state of self-deception, I had to step on that dreaded scale and weigh myself. Of course, I have ignored going on the scale for the longest time possible because what we don't know won't hurt, right? There are also all the deceiving ways I had tried to keep the needle in a favourable position when I did go on the scale. I used to hold my hand against the wall while standing on the scale, as it helped me shave off a few kgs. In hindsight, I now recognise how I deceived myself and that the deception didn't serve me. Why did I lie about my weight to myself? What was I thinking?

But here I was, the new me; I would no longer take shortcuts or deceive myself to help me feel better about myself. I mounted the scale while my heart pounded but was wired to face the truth. The truth was harsh. Harsh. I believe I even shrieked while I looked down at the scale display. The scale had stopped just shy of 140 kgs! I weighed 137 kgs. This whole new me of being truthful to myself didn't feel very considerate of my feelings, but facing reality was the only way forward.

The shock of my reality probably was the main instigator of finally making changes in my life. That evening I sat down behind my laptop and made a list. The list was made up of everything I wanted to achieve. Writing those goals down felt quite abstract because, at the place I was at that time, they seemed inconceivable, but I didn't let that stop me. My main goal was weight loss, of course. The only logical way to achieve it was to consume fewer calories or burn more calories.

I had no idea of my daily calorie intake, so I needed to find a way to register calories as they were consumed. I already had my pedometer, which calculated the calories I burned. My next step was to download an app on my phone, linked to my pedometer, to register every food intake. The app ensured a brilliant track of my calorie intake and, at the same time, deducted the calories I burned from my walks.

I set up the app and entered some personal information which allowed it to suggest my average daily calorie intake to lose weight. To maintain the will to live, I started with small goals. The reality was that I had to lose 60 kgs, but instead of setting such an inconceivable goal, I opted to develop a plan to lose 5 kgs. Once the app was all set up, it suggested a daily calorie intake of fourteen-hundred for me to lose weight. At first, I thought that fourteen-hundred calories sounded all right, but once I initiated entering the foods, I consumed it terrifyingly fast, leaving me with no calories to use.

My habitual pattern of breakfast, lunch and dinner was unattainable to keep up, and I learned the hard way that something had to give. The most challenging part when you start is learning about food's nutritional contents and calories. You'll find yourself in the supermarket reading the nutritional content on the labels of the foods you intend to buy, and you'll learn a thing or two about how deceiving packaging can be. There are a few things that you need to keep an eye on.

Most products have nutritional information on the label because they are obliged to do so by law. You will see that some products also have colour coding on the front; I love them because they make deciding what to buy much more accessible. The colour coding tells you immediately if the food has high (red), medium (amber) or low (green) amounts of fat, saturated fat, sugars, and salt. The greener you find on the label, the healthier the choice and the lower the calories. It's all straightforward; the more beneficial the foods you consume, the lower the calories, and the more you can eat them. Realistically, you want to avoid the reds because that is a red flag saying the food will not do you any good.

The portion sizes displayed on the packaging are usually the manufacturer's recommendation for one portion of the product. The calories, therefore, are worked out based on this portion size. Some labels show the amount of each nutrient in 100 g of the product. This will be given in grams, meaning when you intend to eat 250 g of the product, you must calculate the actual calorie value you will consume.

You'll also quickly learn that some brands of the same product are much higher in calories than others, which has always fascinated me. For example, plain dry spaghetti, do yourself a favour and check the various brands; you will find such a difference in calories between the different brands. You'll also learn that it is essential to use your calories wisely and opt for more filling foods rather than just eating the foods you were used to.

For example, bread. I used to love bread and ate a lot of it.

I've come to a point now where I consider bread a waste of valuable calories in my food intake. This doesn't mean I never eat bread; I still do occasionally, but not how I used to. I used to make myself a sandwich which meant four slices of white bread with two pieces of Leicester cheese in between, and that was just as a snack to top me over to dinner. The total of my little snack on my new calorie counting app tallies up to 510 kcal. If you are on a 1400 kcal daily intake to be able to lose weight, you have already consumed almost half of what you are allowed, and the sandwich wouldn't have filled me anyway. For fewer calories, I could have cooked 250 g of plain spaghetti, with an added drip of olive oil, and have felt fulfilled.

Another eye-opener is processed foods. Most processed foods are very high in calories, so I have eliminated buying ready meals and prepared foods altogether. For example, a jar of tomato pasta sauce of 350 g contains 300 kcal. Instead, I take a teaspoon of olive oil and add one chopped-up onion, two chopped tomatoes and some spices. I let it simmer for a few minutes, then put it through the blender. A delicious pasta sauce contains 86 kcal instead of 300 kcal from the jar. It's all about being smart with your calories and getting the maximum out of them.

Right from the start, it was important to me that I wouldn't feel restricted in any way; neither did I want to feel as if I was starving myself because I knew I wouldn't stick with the plan if I were.

My whole goal was in place, I had my calorie-counting app up and working, my pedometer held me accountable for my daily steps, my sleep monitor told me daily how well (or bad) I had slept, and I had installed an app with hundreds of guided meditations to keep my mind in sync as well. I had all the tools to work with to achieve my goals, so the only one who could mess this up was me. And so, I did.

When I started, I looked for loopholes to make things easier on myself, but I quickly realised that those loopholes set me back eventually. Yes, I have lied to the calorie counter, I have lied to the pedometer, and I have lied to myself repeatedly. The result was that at the end of the week, when I mounted that dreaded scale, I was left disappointed. I would then go on to blame everything under the horizon except myself. Einstein said: "Insanity is doing the same thing repeatedly and expecting different results."

Well, going by that definition, I certainly was insane. I knew exactly what to do to make it work and achieve the results I needed, but still, I kept looking for ways to deceive myself and was left disappointed when it didn't work. The bottom line is that there's no fast track to achieving your goals. There is no easy way out. There is no secret remedy. The only way to get there is to be honest with yourself and not give up, even when you stumble.

I had to find ways to remain honest to keep myself in check. I would go over my calorie-counting app in the evening and search for one thing I did well that I could tap on the back for. Sometimes I had managed to stay under the calorie margin set for me at the end of the day. Sometimes, my pedometer had gone more than thousand steps over the set goal for which I celebrated myself. I just had to find something in my day to highlight, some positive effort that helped me feel good about myself.

Another essential tool I discovered was learning to forgive myself whenever I stumbled. Sometimes I knew consciously that I was consuming something that would set my week back in a big way. As soon as that happened, I would beat myself with it and get frustrated for being so weak. What happened next was that I would feel low because I had beaten down my self-esteem and then crave food to console me; instead of falling into that negative pattern which only made things worse, I learned to forgive myself. The exciting thing about this exercise was that it helped me from making those mistakes. Sometimes I would stand with a chocolate cookie in my hand, about to stuff it in my mouth, and I would think: "Hell no, because then I will have to go and forgive myself again; it's not worth it."

I also found it helpful to set reminders to be truthful to myself. Every week I would add random reminders in my calendar with a notification alert, and then a message would pop up on my phone saying: "Don't fool yourself again!" It did help me, especially in the beginning, when I was still trying to find my way through it all.

At first, it will feel uncomfortable because it is not normal for you; you must adjust and create new habits. For example, I never used to weigh my food; who weighs their food? Although it took an effort to do this, it was a habit I had to create to achieve my goal. I had to get used to weighing everything. Today I don't even think about it; I automatically put my food on the scale and use it to divide even portions when serving it. It's just creating a new habit, and after a while, you get used to them.

Revisiting your goals is essential if something needs to be fixed for you. Remember that this should not be a punishment because when things feel too strenuous, you will resent whatever you are doing and probably give up eventually. For example, in my case, it was vital that I could have dessert after dinner. However, I will favour a lovely dessert with some consistency that isn't ridiculously high in calories. Most evenings, I have a Cornetto ice cream. I knew that including a treat at the end of the day would help me stay motivated. It is possible that after a while, you feel that something doesn't work for you; it might be the timing of your exercise or the nature of the movement. You resent it and simultaneously find yourself looking for excuses to avoid it. It's better to immediately recognise that and nip in it the butt and alter your plans so it feels good to you.

Your goals are not set in stone; they are supposed to be managed by you according to what you need and how it suits you best. This doesn't mean it is a jail-free card to fall back into our old routine, but we know our goals, have our tools, and make them work to our advantage. Remember that this is us building a bridge to a healthier lifestyle.

Let's be truthful here and accept that my old lifestyle didn't serve me well. I had to acknowledge that my old lifestyle had led me down a path where I was no longer comfortable with my body. Even if I deluded myself into thinking I was okay, deep down, I knew and felt I was not. The old lifestyle where I could indulge in whatever I wanted didn't work; it has never worked; it has created a destructive hole where I have found myself being a prisoner of my own body.

The new lifestyle I made was the one I should have always had. It is the lifestyle that was suited for me. I wasn't used to it yet, but I gave it time and found it fit me perfectly. I often find myself wondering why I never realised this before. I have been lying to myself for the past thirty years. I had purposely lured myself away from the lifestyle I should have had because I deluded myself into thinking I needed to consume masses of sugar, thinking that would protect me from fainting in public again. Just writing this down in a sentence seems logical and obvious, but when you are right smack in the middle of it, you can't see it.

That is why we must keep the bigger picture in sight. It

would be best to remind ourselves daily why we are doing this. Picture yourself at your goal weight and think of all the things you will be able to do. You must always keep that image alive as it will stimulate you to stay the course. Recognising how you have deceived yourself in the past is equally important. However hard it is, it is good to say it out loud. It's just a toxic habit that harms us more than it should.

Chapter Six – Getting Out of Our Funk

"If You're Walking Down the Right Path and You're Willing to Keep Walking, Eventually You'll Make Progress." –
Barak Obama.

Calories, calories, calories. You will arrive at a point where you will feel like they're everywhere, staring back at you from food labels, nutrition apps, and diet plans. Whenever you stick something in your mouth, you'll think about the calories you are consuming but more importantly, the number of calories it leaves you with. You cannot just rely on counting calories and neglect your health and well-being. So, you might find yourself in a funk like I did a couple of times during my weight loss journey.

Of course, calorie counting is a helpful tool for weight management and achieving your specific health goals. It's straightforward to tumble into a rabbit hole of counting calories. However, it's essential to approach this with compassion and understanding. Instead of viewing calories as enemies or guilt-inducing digits, I see them as valuable information that empowers me to make informed decisions. As I embarked on my calorie-counting adventure, I surveyed my pantry and discovered a treasure trove of forgotten goodies. Half-eaten bags of potato chips expired cookies, and mystery cans of long-forgotten foods reveal themselves, all eagerly awaiting their caloric reckoning. It was like a game of 'Guess the Calorie Count' as I deciphered the labels and tried to piece together the remnants of my snacking history. Calories alone do not tell the whole story, of course. As I embarked on my journey, I often reminded myself that my worth is not determined by how many calories I consume. I am so much more than a sum of numbers.

Sometimes we must laugh at our occasional mishaps and embrace that all we are doing is trying to find our way in this complex losing weight landscape. I have had a series of mishaps along the way, don't be too hard on yourself. I once went to the cinema with a friend who bought herself a large bag of popcorn to snack on while watching the movie. So as not to be left out of the fun, I scanned the menu looking for something, really anything, that was the least in weight. I thought I had cracked the riddle, and I bought myself a tiny bag of honeycomb balls and snacked on them while my friend was vigorously devouring her popcorn. Later, when I put the calories in the calorie counting app, I discovered that I had consumed more calories with my handful of honeycomb balls than my friend with her massive bag of popcorn. Go figure! Instead of feeling guilty or beating myself over the head in frustration, I laughed... mistakes are bound to happen.

Nutrient density is also vital in understanding the value of our food. Nutrient-dense foods provide many essential vitamins, minerals, and other beneficial compounds while being relatively low in calories. These are the true gems of nourishment that contribute to your well-being. Think of it this way: one-hundred calories of a sugary snack and one-hundred calories of a colourful, fibre-rich salad are not equal. The salad offers a wealth of nutrients that support our body's functions, while the sugary snack provides empty calories without significant nutritional value. By prioritising nutrient-dense foods, we can make every calorie count towards our health and vitality. Tracking calories was something I had to learn with baby steps, and along the way, it gave me an awareness to remain accountable for my intake. I have had times that I thought, I got this, I know what I am doing, and I will put in the calories later. In nine out of ten cases, I went over my calories even though I was convinced I was on top of it in my head. However, it's essential to balance mindful tracking and obsessive monitoring. Remember, you're worth isn't determined by how perfectly you adhere to your calorie goals. Instead, focus on progress, flexibility, and overall well-being. When tracking calories, it's crucial to consider the context. Be mindful of your body's unique needs, listen to your hunger and fullness cues, and practice intuitive eating. While numbers can guide us, especially when we start, they should never override our body's signals. Sometimes, we may exceed our calorie targets, and that's okay.

Life is meant to be savoured, and a healthy relationship with food embraces nourishment and indulgence. Amidst the calorie counting chaos, it's important to maintain sight of the bigger picture: the wisdom of natural, unprocessed foods. Focusing solely on numbers can distract us from the joy of cooking, exploring new flavours, and experiencing the pleasures of food beyond its caloric value. Counting calories involves becoming a Master of Culinary Mathematics. You find yourself calculating the caloric content of each ingredient, weighing, measuring and meticulously jotting down numbers like a mathematician on a mission.

Suddenly, you're summing fractions of a serving, dividing recipes by the number of portions, and discovering that measuring spoons can be your best friends or you're most formidable adversaries. As you delve deeper into calorie counting, you stumble upon surprising revelations. That innocent-looking smoothie you thought was a healthy choice? Surprise! It's hiding alarmingly high-calorie counts due to the sneaky addition of sweeteners and extras. And that seemingly small slice of cake? It could have more calories than an entire meal. The world of hidden calories keeps you on your toes and adds an element of surprise to your culinary calculations. But all joking aside, rather than viewing food as a mere math equation, approach it as a celebration of life. Savour the vibrant colours, the aromas, and the textures of fresh fruits and vegetables. Experiment with herbs, spices, and wholesome ingredients that can transform a simple meal into a feast for the senses. Nurturing your body with nourishing foods goes beyond calories; it nourishes your soul.

Every day I create a dinner from scratch to eat. Fear not, for I too once walked that path of convenience, but I've discovered the truth, the joy of cooking is worth every precious moment spent in the kitchen. I cook fresh food, avoid processed foods, and create incredible dishes that make my family and me happy and fulfilled. The misconception is that cooking processed food is quicker and easier when our busy lives restrict us. Don't worry; I used to think that too. I bought the ready meals, the prepared meals, and dishes that I thought were the only way I could get a meal on the table in my busy life. But cooking fresh food isn't time-consuming; it's another lie we tell ourselves. This daily ritual has become a necessity, a labour of love, and a testament to the transformation that my new lifestyle brings me.

I usually get home by five-thirty p.m. and I aim to have dinner ready for six p.m. so I have a window of thirty minutes. My deceptive mind used to tell me that pre-prepared foods popped in the microwave or the oven was my only option.

Today I go about it differently. Just last evening I walked into the kitchen and put a pot of water on, dropped in some salt, and folded in the pasta once it boiled. In fifteen minutes, my pasta was ready. On the side, I had put one cup of olive oil, one bunch of fresh basil and 50 g of pine nuts with a clove of garlic and a touch of salt through the blender, and one minute later, I had delicious pesto, which I mixed with the pasta. There you have it. In fifteen minutes, I was serving a lovely healthy fresh and tasteful meal for the whole family to enjoy. I even beat the twenty-five minutes that the pre-prepared pizza usually takes when it goes in the oven, which I used to think was the quick and easy way to feed my family.

Once we go down the rabbit hole of calorie tracking, it's easy to overlook the importance of mindful eating. Eating mindfully involves engaging all your senses, savouring each bite, and being fully present. By slowing down and listening to our body, we can establish a deeper connection with our food and our internal hunger and fullness cues. Specifically, eating slower was and still is an ongoing struggle for me. It's most certainly a remanence of my earlier relationship with food and how uncomfortable I would feel around food. I used to gobble down my food at a record speed. These days I really have to watch myself continuously not to gobble but instead eat with mindfulness. When we eat with mindfulness, we become attuned to our body's needs, discovering what truly satisfies us. This allows us to make the right choices, nurturing our bodies and minds. Remember, our worth is not tied to how strictly we adhere to a calorie target but how kindly we treat ourselves.

Dinner these days feels almost like a celebration every evening. I ask Alexa to play music in the background, setting the mood. On the table, I always lit two candles, and with nicely decorated paper napkins, I finish making this experience of having dinner special for everyone. It's small gestures that make a difference in how we eat and how we learn to enjoy consuming our food.

Persistent hunger was one of my struggles with my 1400 kcal/day diet. Consuming fewer calories than what my body was accustomed to triggered feelings of hunger and food cravings all the time. I tend to joke about this when someone asks me how I lost all that weight; I tend to reply: "By being hungry." It wasn't all that dramatic if I am being honest with you. Listen, I have to be honest, and we will feel hungry significantly when drastically dropping our calorie intake. I went from an average of 5000-8000 kcal/day to 1400 kcal/day. You don't need to be a rocket scientist to know that that shift will leave some marks. When hunger strikes, it can be challenging to resist the urge to indulge in high-calorie foods, so that is a significant bridge we must push ourselves over, and it won't be easy for at least two to three weeks. When our body adjusts to our new calorie intake regime, the hunger will quiet down, and things will get easier.

There are a couple of pitfalls to watch out for, however. Firstly, there is the issue of boredom. Boredom creates a need for food within us. I haven't quite figured out the logic behind this yet, but when we are bored, we reach for a snack. The best way to conquer that is to stick a piece of gum in my mouth instead when I feel bored. At least I am chewing on something. I suppose the best way is to find something to engage in that keeps our minds occupied to distract ourselves from hunger. Going for a walk, reading a book, doing a puzzle, or conversing with someone. Picking up the phone and calling a friend. We can reduce the urge to snack out of boredom or habit by redirecting our focus.

Sometimes hunger pangs can also be mistaken for thirst, which is quite confusing. Before reaching for a snack, I drink a glass of water and wait a few minutes to see if my hunger subsides. Often warm drinks also give me a feeling of fulfilment when hungry.

There's also the stress factor that can sometimes trigger us to think we are hungry, which consequently makes us pick up food. Emotional or stress-related eating is a tricky one and often leads to overconsumption of calories. There are alternative ways to manage stress, such as practising meditation, deep breathing exercises or engaging in non-seated fun. We must always remain alert to our stressors to minimise the temptation to use food as a coping mechanism.

Eating out can also pose a real challenge when we are calorie counting. We will find ourselves decoding menu descriptions like a detective trying to crack a case. What exactly is 'lightly dressed' in a salad? How many calories are hiding in that 'artisanal' bread? And can the waiter tell you the precise calorie count of the dish you're eyeing? Sometimes, the restaurant riddles leave us scratching our heads and resorting to our best guesswork. There's no perfect solution for dining out, although some apps include the calorie count for certain restaurant dishes, and then it becomes easier.

In most cases, it's just a guessing game. Whenever I couldn't escape a restaurant dinner, I would call it a cheat day and drop the counting for the day. Unless, for some reason, we have to eat out daily, I wouldn't make a big deal about eating out occasionally. Relax and enjoy.

Another pitfall I found was navigating the snack aisles at the store. I found this became quite the adventure. We will find ourselves standing in front of a wall of colourful packages, deciphering nutrition labels. Low-fat, low-carb, high-fibre, gluten-free—the options seem endless. It's a comedy of errors as we try to choose a snack that fits our calorie goals while avoiding an accidental sugar rush or a fat overload.

Ah, and then there are the dreaded misplaced decimal points, the bane of every calorie counter's existence. One moment of distraction, one tiny slip, and suddenly, that innocent tablespoon of peanut butter has transformed into a calorie bomb. It's a lesson in attention to detail as we learn to double-check our calculations and avoid the calorie-counting pitfalls that lie in wait.

It's not all gloom and doom. After all, we are pretty lucky because we live in a health-conscious era today, so managing our caloric intake has never been easier. All foods provide clear labels with all their values visibly marked. Especially in the beginning, it will require us to read all the labels, and it might take some time to get on the right track, but we should not get discouraged. Like anything, it's a learning process. It might start as a struggle but trust me, it will become almost second nature before you know it. Over time, you will understand the calorie contents of all the foods you regularly use and become a walking, talking calorie master.

Creating a well-balanced meal plan is also essential. Especially when we are learning how to stay within the 1400 kcal/day available. When setting up our plan, divide the daily calorie intake among meals and snacks to ensure consistent energy distribution throughout the day.

Calorie counting teaches us the delicate art of finding balance. It's a dance between indulgence and discipline, between enjoying our favourite treats and making healthier choices. We learn it's not about deprivation but about finding moderation and creating a sustainable lifestyle. It's a humourous tightrope act as we navigate the calorie tightrope, occasionally teetering but always finding our balance.

The best way is to aim for nutrient-dense foods that offer essential vitamins, minerals, and macronutrients while being mindful of calorie content. Portion control also plays a vital role in managing caloric intake. Managing my 1400 kcal/day diet required knowledge, planning and discipline. By understanding my caloric needs, planning balanced meals, practising portion control, prioritising nutrient-dense foods, tracking caloric intake, and incorporating my non-seated fun of course, I effectively managed my information while achieving my health and wellness goals. Maintaining a healthy lifestyle is not a temporary phase you have to plough through, but it will be a continuous journey, and adapting to our needs and preferences is essential for long-term success.

Chapter Seven – The Highs, the Lows, the Mistakes

"Experience is Simply the Name We Give Our Mistakes." –
Oscar Wilde.

Embarking on this lifestyle change felt like being on a rollercoaster ride filled with all the highs, and the lows, and mind you, there will be a few comical moments as well. The funny moments are mainly our unavoidable mistakes, so I have learned to laugh them off.

Few experiences rival the exhilaration and sheer motivation that courses through you when embarking on a new journey. Like your first day at school, you are all set up in your new uniform and backpack filled with new books and pens. It feels like a brisk, refreshing breeze on a bright, sunlit morning, invigorating and full of promise.

Just like that first day at school I now stood at the threshold of my adventure, armed with a dazzling set of brand-new, vibrant containers that held the promise of wholesome meals. My refrigerator, a treasure trove of crisp, colourful produce, offers me endless possibilities. And as I reach for that early morning snack, a collage of inspiring quotes adorns my fridge, serving as daily reminders of my aspirations. In this moment, I was all ready to go, ready to conquer uncharted territories. This euphoric high sets the stage for the thrilling journey that awaited me, where every meal, every choice and every step is a vibrant stroke on the canvas of my journey.

Be prepared to encounter an unexpected side effect after eating healthier foods and losing weight. Suddenly we will find that we have boundless energy! We will find ourselves zipping through our to-do list, signing up for every exercise class available, and even considering starting a side hustle. Who knew that a simple change in diet and loss of weight could turn us into a human Energizer bunny? But that is what happened to me in those two first week. I felt unstoppable. This high sets the tone for the whole adventure ahead, and there will be moments when we have lost significant weight and will experience a 'Sudden Burst of Energy' High.

In reality, though, the scale might only sometimes reflect our efforts, but then embrace the non-scale victories that will provide us with a much-needed boost. Suddenly, we find that we are fitting into those jeans hiding in the back of our closet, which is such a great feeling. Out of the blue, we receive random compliments from friends and family about our glowing complexion, and we soon find that these little wins make it all worth it.

A huge one is when you notice that all your clothes have become oversized. Looking back at it today I cannot quite remember this process because I was always used to wearing oversized clothes. I do recall one day when I put on one of my favourite dresses and it felt as if I was a child wearing adult clothes. That was the moment when I knew I had to let go of my oversized clothes. After a long time of being stuck in my comfort zone of online clothes shopping, I decided to venture into the world of in-store clothing shopping again. It was like stepping into a whole new dimension!

I vividly remember the first time I walked into a clothing

store to buy a coat after my weight loss. The feeling was surreal. I remember it was a crisp sunny autumn day as I approached the inviting doors of a clothing store. The bell chimed softly as I stepped inside, and little did I know that this would mark a significant moment in my weight loss journey. As I walked further into the store, the racks of coats stretched out before me with abundant possibilities.

My anticipation was palpable because a sense of frustration and disappointment had marked my shopping trips for so many years. Sizing charts and dress codes had felt more like barriers than guidelines. But on this particular day, something was different. A newfound sense of confidence and determination coursed through my veins. Then came the moment of truth: I decided to challenge myself and started by trying on a size sixteen. It felt like a daring leap, a leap of faith in myself. Would it fit? Could I really wear something so beautifully tailored? These thoughts swirled in my mind as I approached the fitting room with my chosen coat in hand.

Inside that small, well-lit room, I slipped the coat over my shoulders, my heart racing with anticipation. It slid on the coat effortlessly like it had been custom-made for me. A tear of joy welled up in my eye as I twirled in front of the mirror. That surreal feeling was overwhelming. The reflection staring back at me was a testament to my hard work, dedication, and unwavering commitment to becoming the best version of myself.

At that moment, the size of the coat didn't matter as much as the size of the smile on my face. It was exhilarating to realise that I could embrace fashion, confidently select an outfit, and truly revel in the simple pleasure of finding a coat that fit perfectly. It was a small victory, but it symbolised a monumental journey of self-discovery, self-acceptance, and the boundless possibilities.

Trying on that size sixteen coat was nerve-wracking. It had been ages since I wore anything that size. When I put it on, it was comically oversized. I felt like a kid playing dress-up in their parent's clothes. It gave me this delightful, giddy feeling. But here's the kicker: the size I was sceptical about if it would fit me was too big for me. I was blown away. I mean, seriously mind blown. Next up was a size fourteen, which I was convinced would be too small. I mean, I hadn't fit into a size fourteen in over thirty years. But lo and behold, it turned out that even this size was still too big for me. The coat hung over my waist, and the sleeves drooped over my hands. I couldn't believe my eyes. Feeling lightheaded and slightly in disbelief, I gathered my courage and tried on a size twelve coat. And guess what? It fitted like a glove. Perfectly. My mind was completely blown! I sprinted to the checkout, paid for that coat, and practically danced out of the store. Once I found a quiet spot in a little side alley, I sat down, leaned against a wall, and let the tears flow. Tears of happiness, relief, disbelief, and joy all rolled into one.

I had been wearing a size twenty-four or even larger before this moment. Walking out of that store with a size twelve coat was indescribable. It's not about being hung up on sizes; it's about the incredible experience of walking into a store, picking something off the rack, and having it fit. It's the kind of story you hear from others, but I never imagined it could happen to me. This experience is something I'll cherish for the rest of my life. This transformative moment on my journey was only the beginning of the change to come, and the familiar markers of my past self soon began to blur and fade away.

Embracing this new lifestyle was also an extraordinary journey filled with delightful culinary discoveries. It's as if I've embarked on a grand expedition into the world of food, and every day is a new adventure. One of the most remarkable experiences have been my trips to the farmer's market. There, I've been enchanted by the vibrant selection of fruits and vegetables on display. It's like stepping into a living, breathing palette of colours and flavours. I've learned to appreciate the art of transforming humble zucchini into tantalising spirals, turning cauliflower into velvety, creamy soups, and creating scrumptious chia seed puddings. Who would have thought that healthy eating could be this delicious and full of culinary exploration?

Just the other day I celebrated that it had been three years since I last bought a ready-made meal, and I will be honest with you, just looking at ready meals in the supermarket now makes my stomach turn. The idea of reverting to my old habits of eating prepared meals and indulging in pizzas is utterly unimaginable.

In this fast-paced, ever-evolving world, there's a secret ingredient to happiness that's been hiding in plain sight all along, healthy food. As I look back on my remarkable journey towards a healthier me, I can't help but marvel at how this simple change in diet has not only transformed my physical well-being but has also sprinkled a generous dose of joy into every facet of my life.

Imagine for a moment a world where the bustling streets are lined with vibrant fruit stands and bustling markets offering the freshest, most nourishing foods. The aroma of ripe fruits and colourful vegetables fills the air, invigorating our senses. In this world, people aren't just mindful of what they eat; they savour the journey of selecting ingredients and crafting wholesome meals.

You see, healthy eating isn't just about shedding pounds or fitting into smaller clothing sizes; it's about embracing life with open arms and a radiant smile. It's about discovering the joy of preparing meals from scratch, experimenting with flavours, and relishing the satisfaction of a well-balanced plate.

But it goes even further. When we nourish our bodies with the right nutrients, something remarkable happens within us. Our moods lift, our spirits soar, and we become beacons of positivity in a world that often seems to be teetering on the edge of chaos. It's like a symphony of happiness, each bite composing a note of contentment, and every meal a harmonious melody that resonates through our days.

In this ideal world, where healthy eating is a way of life, there's a noticeable shift in the collective consciousness. People are more patient, more compassionate and less prone to the anger and tumult that often plague our society. It's as if a cloud of serenity has settled over the world, allowing us to see the beauty in every moment and appreciate the connections we share.

Healthy food, you see, isn't just fuel for the body; it's nourishment for the soul. It's a reminder that taking care of ourselves can have a ripple effect, touching the lives of those around us and ultimately transforming the fabric of our world. So, the next time you savour a crisp salad or relish a juicy piece of fruit, remember that you're not just nourishing your body but contributing to a happier, more harmonious world for us all.

I look back at my initial hesitation when I began this journey and the mourning process of leaving behind my old lifestyle, and I find it comical. What was I thinking back then?

Today, I don't see my lifestyle change as a loss any more. Instead, I consider it a fortunate escape from a lifestyle that felt like a one-way ticket to a health crisis. The contrast between then and now is so vivid that it's like living in a different world altogether.

Ah, the journey I've been on was not always lined with rose

petals, though. I promised you there would be no secrets between us, so here it goes. There were those nights when the siren call of late-night cravings strikes, and suddenly, I would find myself drawn to the glow of the refrigerator, on a quest to satisfy my craving.

In those moments, I reach for a carrot, and as I crunch into it, I can't help but wish it could magically transform into a slice of pizza. It's like a little battle of desires happening right there in the kitchen. But sometimes, I must admit, those late-night cravings get the better of me. My hand reaches for the cheese instead of the carrot, and that slice of pizza seems to win the skirmish.

But here's the thing: it's all part of the journey. We're only human, after all. In those moments when the cravings win, we must show compassion. It shouldn't become a regular occurrence, but we must allow ourselves to occasionally stumble. Trust me, it happens to everyone, and there's absolutely no shame in it.

When those moments come, it's essential to remember that tomorrow is a new day. We can pick ourselves up again, recommit to our goals, and move forward with renewed determination. Challenges and temptations will always be there along the way, but it's how we respond to them that defines our journey. So, let's be kind to ourselves, knowing that every stumble is just a slight detour on the road to our healthier and happier selves.

Let me tell you about that day I had diligently packed my beautiful, Instagram-worthy salad for lunch, complete with an assortment of colourful veggies and a homemade dressing. As I sat down with my friends at the park, they went to the kiosk and ordered their juicy burgers, crispy fries, and decadent desserts.

Suddenly, my salad looked a little less exciting. I caved in and got some crispy fries to add to my salad. Sometimes we must stop to see the whole picture before digging our heels too deep in the sand. That day at the park was all about enjoying precious time spent with dear friends while sharing a picnic on the lawn. There will be times like that that we have to allow ourselves to enjoy, so I did and threw in the towel that day. Just be aware that it doesn't become a repeatable offence.

Another thing that I have learned, and also the people close to me, is that hunger can transform even the most composed person into a raging, ferocious beast. Sometimes, I have snapped at my loved ones for no apparent reason, I have found myself glaring at innocent pedestrians who dared to walk too slowly, and I confess that on many occasions, I have been eyeing my partner's sandwich with envy and irrational anger. It's incredible how hunger can turn us into temporary monsters. It's not a pleasant experience when I'm watching someone eating a copious meal while I have to restrain myself to my low-calorie plate. Murderous thoughts have passed my mind. It's all part of the process. It's okay. Nobody got harmed in the process.

We must be prepared to the fact that mistakes will happen; it doesn't matter how diligently we track our calories while meticulously measuring each portion. Somewhere along the way, we might accidentally input the quantity for an entire cake slice instead of a single bite-sized piece. Suddenly, our calorie count is sky-high, and we can't help but wonder if we accidentally consumed the caloric equivalent of an entire bakery.

There will be times when we proudly prepare a healthy dinner for ourselves, carefully weighing each ingredient and following the recipe to a T. But just as we sit down to enjoy our creation, our well-meaning spouse surprises us with a plate of fresh-out-of-the-oven chocolate chip cookies. The aroma fills the air, and our diet plans are temporarily derailed. We might meticulously plan our meals for the week, creating a detailed grocery list and stocking up on all the necessary ingredients. But as we unpack the groceries and put everything away, we realise we forgot the crucial element for our dinner, an essential component that cannot be substituted. It's a terrifying moment when we realise how a momentary lapse in memory can throw off our entire meal plan.

The lifestyle change adventure takes us through a whirlwind of highs, lows, and apparent mistakes and lapses. While the journey may have challenges and self-doubt, embracing humour is essential. Remember to celebrate the joys, laugh at the lows, and learn from our mistakes. After all, it is not just about achieving our health and wellness goals; it's also about finding joy along the way. So, keep your sense of humour intact, enjoy the ride, and don't forget to savour that occasional slice of pizza!

Chapter Eight – New-Found Confidence

"Believe You Can, and You're Halfway There." – *Theodore Roosevelt.*

Early on in my journey, while still learning and researching, I came across this ancient Greek mythological story which made a tremendous impact on me.

It's the story of a young man named Perseus who exemplifies the transformation from self-doubt to self-confidence. Perseus was the son of Danaë, a princess imprisoned in a tower by her father, King Acrisius, due to a prophecy that foretold her child would one day kill him. The young Perseus grew up in captivity, feeling powerless and trapped.

Perseus decided to rescue his mother from her tower prison. Armed with determination and a belief in himself, he set out on a dangerous quest.

Perseus encountered numerous challenges on his journey, including the monstrous Gorgon sisters, among whom Medusa was the most feared. Medusa's gaze turned anyone looking into her eyes into stone. Perseus realised that to rescue his mother, he had to face Medusa.

He embarked on this seemingly impossible mission with the help of divine gifts: a mirrored shield to avoid Medusa's gaze, a pair of winged sandals for agility, and a magical sword. Armed with these tools and a newfound sense of purpose, Perseus confronted Medusa.

The battle was fierce, but Perseus's determination and resourcefulness prevailed. He used the mirrored shield to navigate Medusa's deadly gaze and severed her head with the magical sword. From Medusa's lifeless body, a winged horse named Pegasus was born, and Perseus claimed her head as a weapon.

With Medusa's head as his prize, Perseus returned to his mother's tower, freeing her from captivity. Perseus's journey had transformed him from a self-doubting young man into a self-confident hero who had faced his deepest fears and conquered them.

Perseus's story reminded me that self-confidence often emerges when confronting our inner demons and tackling life's challenges head-on. Like Perseus, we may feel trapped or powerless at times, but by believing in ourselves, acquiring the necessary skills, and facing our fears, we can transform into heroes of our own stories. It's a reminder that self-confidence is not an innate quality but a trait that can be developed through courage, determination, and the willingness to confront the most daunting of challenges.

Losing a substantial amount of weight is an extraordinary accomplishment. This story is a testament to my personal transformation's power in a world where self-acceptance and confidence are often elusive. I shared my story because I want to empower you, so you get to experience this transformation too.

My journey began with my decision to reclaim my life and probably save my life while I was at it. I never intended to lose 60 kgs when I started this journey because that seemed inconceivable. I would have lost 10 kgs. That would have been such an accomplishment for me. Somewhere along this journey, goalposts got moved, unachievable became achievable and doubts transformed into little miracles. Little did I know that this physical endeavour would lead me towards finding newfound confidence, self-love and a deep understanding of my inner strength.

Those are the things that diet books don't tell you. I never contemplated how the loss of weight would make me feel or make me think. It never crossed my mind that there would be a significant shift in my behaviour towards myself and outward to the world.

In the distant past, I was once a vibrant young woman full of dreams and aspirations, living an active life without hesitation. As my story goes, I went through some unfortunate experiences that led me to land where I found myself confined within the shadows of my body. As the kilos piled on over the years, I literary became a stranger to myself. From that moment onwards, I was plagued by self-doubt and lacked the confidence to pursue my passions. It's as if I just aborted my true self and took on the role of the new obese me with all the consequences that came with it. Daily tasks became arduous, and the whispers of judgment echoed in my mind continuously. The more weight I piled on, the further my self-esteem eroded.

It was a day etched in the annals of my memory, a day that would inadvertently set the stage for a profound transformation. The world was in the throes of an unprecedented lockdown, and like many, I found myself confined to the sanctuary of my home, seeking solace in the dusty pages of old photo albums. Little did I know that within those pages lay a portal to my past, a revelation that would spark a journey of self-discovery.

As I flipped through the faded photographs of cherished moments and long-forgotten adventures, one image, in

96

particular, caught my eye. There she was, a younger version of myself, an energetic and carefree soul, radiant with confidence that seemed to leap off the glossy paper. Yet, as I gazed at the photograph, I couldn't help but feel like a distant observer, disconnected from the vibrant person staring back at me. Memories of that time, the emotions, and the vitality of that younger self had become an enigma, a puzzle I struggled to piece together. What was it like to be her, to embrace life with such gusto, to revel in the excitement of each day? I was left grappling with these questions, a sense of nostalgia washing over me like a tidal wave.

But in the midst of that nostalgia, a glimmer of hope emerged. It was a profound realisation that, once upon a time, I had been a healthy, happy, and vibrant individual. That photograph served as a silent testament to a version of myself that had been buried beneath the weight of time and life's challenges. It was a whisper from the past, reminding me of the potential for a brighter future.

This realisation, though subtle, was like a spark in the darkness, igniting a flame of determination within me. It was a call to action, a summons to reclaim the essence of who I once was. And as fate would have it, it was during this time of introspection that I stumbled upon the wisdom of Ricky Gervais, when I heard him speak those enlightening words on that random podcast.

They say that miracles work in mysterious ways, and indeed they do. The act of stumbling upon that photograph of my younger self, combined with the serendipity of discovering the Podcast with Ricky Gervais making that seemingly banal statement, marked the genesis of a journey that would ultimately redefine my life. It was a journey back to health, happiness and the vibrant spirit that had long lain dormant within me, waiting to be rekindled.

So, in the labyrinthine tapestry of life, it was this seemingly chance encounter with my own past that set the stage for a remarkable transformation, reminding me that even in the most unexpected moments, the universe has a way of guiding us towards the path we were always meant to tread.

After hearing Ricky make it sound so simple and attainable, I made that life-changing decision: I would shed weight. I hadn't yet determined how much weight I would lose because I wanted to play it safe to avoid disappointing myself. Still, I aimed to lose enough weight that would allow me to rediscover the person I was meant to be.

Armed with a newfound resolve, I embarked on my lifestyle journey. It was not an easy path, and I must confess that there have been times when I thought I wouldn't make it. I encountered the obvious torturous physical challenges and many moments of self-doubt along the way.

Yet, with each milestone I reached, my confidence grew. As the numbers on the scale decreased, my transformation extended far beyond my physical appearance. I shed not only kilos but also layers of self-limiting beliefs and insecurities. My perspective shifted, and I gradually began to view myself with the kindness and compassion I deserved. Along the process, I slowly embraced my journey as an opportunity for personal growth and self-discovery.

Again, they don't tell you this in diet books, but I soon realised that with my newfound confidence radiating from within, I began to engage more fully with the world around me. It's baby steps; they aren't enormous shifts then, but I felt my confidence grow with small baby steps.

Initially, I shied away from exercising in public, so when I would go out for my 'non-seated fun' walks, I would always be dressed as if I were going to the shops. That gradually changed, and I began wearing leggings and a t-shirt for the same 'non-seated fun' walk that I used to do all dolled up.

I found myself pursuing activities that I had once deemed impossible. For example, I would join my daughter and her partner on walks involving climbs I would never have undertaken in a million years. I'd certainly have given a hard pass on any walk that wasn't flat-level.

I joined them in a rowing boat on a lake once, again an undertaking I would never have dreamt of doing before. In the past, I would have been worried I'd capsize the boat.

I recently joined people on a three-hour hike in the middle of nowhere, which was unimaginable in my old state. My energy and vitality became contagious, attracting positive influences and I fostered deeper connections.

My journey towards self-confidence led me to a profound realisation that true transformation begins with self-love. True self-confidence begins with kindness towards oneself. I began challenging my negative beliefs, replacing them with affirmations of self-worth and acceptance. With every act of self-love, a flicker of confidence began to ignite within me.

It's a steep hill, but I shed my self-loathing and embraced my individuality wholeheartedly. I taught myself to appreciate my unique qualities and talents, recognising that comparison to others only stifled my growth. I celebrated my accomplishments, no matter how small, and soon recognised that I had something valuable to offer the world.

Even better, I realised that I had value. For more than thirty years, I had felt lesser than everyone because of my weight. I had become accustomed to pushing myself to the background in any situation. It meant that I had to push myself out of my comfort zone daily, but a whole new world opened up to me when I did. I immersed myself in self-care practices, nourishing my mind, body and soul. My daily affirmations and gratitude exercises became my allies, gradually erasing the scars of self-criticism and paving the way for a more fulfilling life.

As I emerged from the shadows, I found myself basking in the warm embrace of my light. I truly radiated confidence, and my presence grew captivating. My transformation also inspired those around me; even strangers would stop me in the street and proclaim that I looked good.

Looking back at my whole journey from the shadows to the light is truly a testament to the indomitable spirit that we have within each of us. Through perseverance, self-belief, and a relentless pursuit of self-love, I shed a significant amount of weight and discovered my true worth, my true self.

This is probably why I felt it was important to write my story. I can only strive that my story stands as a beacon of hope, reminding us of all that within the darkness lies the potential for an extraordinary transformation and a journey towards newfound confidence and a life lived authentically.

Chapter Nine – Life on the Other Side

"I Attribute My Success to This: I Never Gave or Took Any Excuse." – Florence Nightengale.

Let's begin with the notion that we all should be aware that dieting has a darker side, so we can be vigilant not to fall into its trap.

In a world where weight loss is often celebrated as a triumph, the hidden complexities of this journey can sometimes be neglected by the allure of the scale's downward arrow.

Firstly, avoid any 'Extreme Diet' Trap. Imagine going from a leisurely stroll to a marathon overnight. That's what extreme diets are. They promise quick results but often leave you miserable and craving everything you can't have. Remember, slow and steady wins the race!

Another one to avoid is the 'All or Nothing' Attitude. Picture this, you're on a diet, and you accidentally eat one cookie. Instead of forgiving yourself, you eat the entire cookie jar, thinking, "I'll start again tomorrow." Don't let one slip-up sabotage your entire journey. It's okay to indulge occasionally; get back on track the next day.

Avoid the 'Overcomplication' conundrum. When you follow a diet plan with ingredients you can't even pronounces and a meal prep routine that takes as long as a cooking show, you set yourself up for failure. Keep it simple! Focus on whole foods, portion control, and balanced meals. You don't need a culinary degree to eat healthily.

The one that I had to watch out for was the 'Scale Obsession' sinkhole. Imagine stepping on the scale every day, hoping for a miracle. Weight fluctuates naturally, and daily weigh-ins can drive you mad. Use the scale as a tool, not a torture device. Measure your progress over weeks, not hours.

Surround yourself with a support system, whether it's friends, family, or online communities. They can provide motivation, advice, and a shoulder to lean on when the going gets tough.

Remember, your weight loss journey is a story of resilience, determination, and self-discovery. By avoiding any pitfalls and embracing a balanced, sustainable approach, you can inspire others to embark on their successful journeys.

Try not to focus exclusively on weight loss because that can be a treacherous path, leading to a precarious imbalance in our well-being.

On a psychological level, there's a certain sensation of 'success' that our culture engrains in us as we watch the numbers on the scale decrease. However, what our culture often neglects to teach us is how to navigate the inevitable plateau. This uncharted territory can trigger a vicious cycle of self-doubt and feelings of inadequacy.

Dieting, as it restricts calorie intake and modifies eating habits, can directly impact the happy chemicals in our brain, such as serotonin and dopamine. This alteration can significantly affect our mood, leaving us more susceptible to feelings of anxiety and depression.

Be prudent that your quest for weight loss doesn't transcend a mere desire; and turn into an all-consuming obsession or even an addiction, with consequences that will ripple through to your personal relationships and your psychological health.

I remember reading a story about a woman whose story was similar to mine. She was once a vivacious woman in her twenties, but after an unhappy marriage, she found herself on the doorstep of obesity. She went on a diet and lost all the weight she had been unhappy about. Then she was trapped by the siren call of the 'thin ideal' when she saw images of the iconic model Twiggy which convinced her that she needed to be thinner to feel attractive again. Her journey took a dangerous turn as she embarked on a path of extreme restriction.

She began to starve herself, reducing her meals to just yoghurt for breakfast and lunch. She pushed herself to the limit by incorporating an aerobics class into her daily routine. Yet, instead of feeling like a beautiful model, weight loss only made her very miserable. Caught in a relentless cycle of self-judgment and dissatisfaction, she was trapped in a never-ending loop of believing something was fundamentally wrong with her. This harrowing tale serves as a stark reminder that the messages of weight loss, often woven intricately into the fabric of our culture, can lead individuals down a treacherous path of self-deprecation and despair. The relentless pursuit of thinness is detrimental to our culture, but I have pursued happiness and well-being above all.

Once I reached that point where I had finally achieved the unimaginable, a victory dance extravaganza to commemorate my incredible achievement was certainly not out of place.

I have shamelessly bathed myself in compliments and admiration from friends and family. But as the confetti settles and the music fades, you will soon realise that the journey continues after reaching the weight loss goal.

When you thought losing weight was tricky, I must disappoint you because it's not over yet. It will be a lifelong commitment to staying on track and maintaining your newfound healthier lifestyle.

So don't delete your calorie-counting app just as yet. You'll most likely be watching portions and counting calories for the foreseeable future. I learned that staying on track is more accessible when surrounded by supportive people who don't lead you into temptation every turn of the way.

I know the deal and what it takes to maintain my weight. It's still a challenging place to be, and I have found myself indulging a bit too much and gaining a few kilos here and there, but I am aware that I cannot let this fabulous new me slip through my fingers. It truly isn't worth it.

From substituting cauliflower for pizza crust to blending kale into colourful smoothies, I navigate the world of healthy eating with a light-hearted approach, ultimately discovering a balance between nourishing meals and the occasional indulgence. It is not about perfection but about having fun and finding joy.

You will encounter moments of self-doubt, temptation and rare setbacks. But with a light-hearted and positive mindset, you can overcome these challenges. I embrace my affirmations daily; I have vision boards filled with inspiring quotes and images and surround myself with uplifting messages to stay on track. The power of positivity has become my secret weapon and has helped me navigate the emotional journey of staying on track with laughter, resilience and a can-do attitude. Sharing my story of transformation and inspiring others to embark on their journeys of health and self-discovery also keeps me accountable.

Life, on the other side, has been an eye-opening journey for me. Things have changed; I have changed, my appearance has changed, and my life has changed.

I wasn't consciously aware of the biggest eye-opener that trumps all when I embarked on this journey. I was oblivious to it, to be honest and I feel that it takes a trip to the other side to see it truly. I was aware of my self-image and the subsequent low self-esteem attached to it.

I was fully aware of how obese people are subjected to societal biases, stereotypes and unequal treatment. I was fully aware of how obese individuals encounter harsh societal judgment, experience weight stigma and are shamelessly associated with laziness, lack of discipline, and poor health. When I was obese, I frequently encountered stigmatising attitudes and discriminatory behaviours. It was all part of being me. I had my share of derogatory remarks, ridicule and bullying based on my weight. This mistreatment occurred in various settings, in the workplace, at healthcare facilities and even within personal relationships.

Such experiences led to me feeling ashamed, and of course, they ignited my low self-esteem in full swing, which encouraged my social isolation.

I once had a male friend said to me jokingly, "You have a pretty face, but with a body like that, you will never get laid." I laughed out loud with him while I was silently slowly dying inside. After that, I didn't keep him in my circle of friends much longer. Those judgements and the brutal treatment I were used to. We know it exists if we are all honest with ourselves.

Today, the perception and treatment of individuals based on their weight is real. What I never realised, though, is that on the other side, as a non-obese person, suddenly, people see me, people notice me, people respect me and people treat me with dignity.

Non-obese people get very fair treatment in society. It took me shedding off over 60 kgs to see and experience those significant changes in how others perceive and interact with me. Usually, it is pretty subtle and mostly unintentional and innocent. Still, when you are obese, you get overlooked, you are grey, you are excluded, and you are treated differently to others. The first moment this blatantly stared me in the face was when one day, when I was no longer obese, and I walked out of Starbucks, a man held the door open for me. Again, this may sound like an everyday occurrence for the outsider, but to me; it was an experience I hadn't had for as long as I could remember. Then I started noticing that cars would stop to let me cross the road, random people would greet me in the street, and people would treat me friendly and generously.

Suddenly people would just come and take the seat next to me on the bus, while before, that would only happen if all other seats had been taken. It is sad to admit, but I hadn't experienced these things when I was obese.

The reality is that it is just how our society works; society sees and treats obese differently. It's subtle and not as flagrant as the guy telling me I will never get laid, but it's there all right. It happens all around us without us being consciously aware of it. No matter who you are or how good your intentions are, the world treats obese people differently.

Today my memory of being obese is still fresh, I can recognise and see it. But I didn't realise that non-obese people got a different treatment in general and were received on a different level than I was as an obese woman.

We live in a complex world where I've come to understand something important. People often don't receive the fair and equal treatment they deserve in our society, and that's genuinely disheartening. It's not about judgment based on appearances; it's about recognising that everyone should have an equal shot at life, regardless of factors like body shape or size.

On a personal note, my own transformation has been significant, but deep down, I've realised that the woman I used to be still resides within me. Even as I stand in front of the mirror and see my new self, there are moments when my mind insists on projecting an image that doesn't quite match reality. It's almost like my past self is still there, casting a shadow of doubt and surprise.

My mind plays tricks on me, reminding me that fully embracing my new body is a journey that requires time and a healthy dose of humour. As I observe my new physique, the ghost of my former self looms large, resulting in moments of disbelief and a perpetual double-take.

The other day people were taking pictures in a group setting, and afterwards, I looked at one of the pictures and didn't see myself in the picture. I had to look closely and then realised that the blond woman in the back of the group was me. I didn't recognise me. I didn't expect me to look so vanilla, blending in with the rest of the women in the picture.

Somehow my mind clings to the belief that I am still the same size I used to be. In the depths of my mind, an inner monologue persists, whispering reminders of my former struggles with weight. It insists I'm just one bite away from regaining all those kilos. This internal dialogue sometimes becomes a source of amusement as I navigate the separation between my current healthy habits and the lingering mindset of an overweight individual.

Let's talk about something relatable, the quirky ways our

minds work. I often find myself in amusing situations, gently reminding myself of how far I've come, even if my mind occasionally detours.

In social settings, my mind sometimes plays a playful game of comparisons, making me feel like the 'larger person' in a crowd of slender figures. Despite my transformation, I'll stand beside someone and still have moments where I feel like I occupy more space than I actually do.

It's a whimsical dance, really. I chuckle to myself and remind myself that my mind's perception isn't always in sync with reality. In these moments, I embrace the humour, understanding that beauty and self-worth come in all shapes and sizes. As I navigate life with my changed body and a mind that occasionally recalls my past,

I've come to terms with the fact that personal growth is an ongoing journey. I've accepted that my mind's perception may always carry traces of my past, but that doesn't define who I am today. Each day, I nurture self-compassion and celebrate my progress. I let these quirks and light-hearted moments weave themselves into my story. In the whimsical world of self-perception, it's not unusual to sometimes feel like the 'larger' person in a slimmer, healthier body.

I have openly described my weight loss journey and my personal transformation in this book just as I have experienced it. Just realise we all experience different things differently, and my journey most likely won't be yours. All I can hope for, though, is that maybe somewhere in this book, you will find your 'aha' moment that helps you discover your options and possibilities for your journey in transformation.

As we reach the end of this book, I feel happy you've joined me on this adventure of knowledge and inspiration. Throughout this book, I've aimed to ignite the spark within you, awaken your curiosity, and empower you with the tools needed to achieve greatness.

Now, as we part ways, I want to leave you with a heartfelt message of encouragement. I sincerely hope that I have ignited a fire within your soul and that you find yourself brimming with newfound enthusiasm and determination.

Remember, the world is vast, filled with infinite possibilities waiting to be discovered by those who dare to dream and believe in themselves. You possess within you an immense well of potential, waiting to be tapped into and unleashed upon the world.

I hope I have provided you with the knowledge, inspiration, and guidance to embark on a path that leads you to more than you have ever dreamed of. May you surpass the boundaries of your imagination and shatter the limits that society and self-doubt may have placed upon you.

In the grand tapestry of life, we are all interconnected, and the experiences we accumulate shape our destinies and the world around us. I hope that you seize every opportunity, take risks, and learn from every triumph and setback, for it is through these experiences that you will grow, evolve, and become the best version of yourself.

Just as I have been fortunate enough to witness breathtaking moments, explore the uncharted territories of knowledge, and savour the fruits of relentless determination, I want you to experience the same. Life is an extraordinary tapestry waiting for you to weave your unique thread into its fabric.

So, my dear reader, change your life today, chase your dreams and never let self-doubt hold you back. Believe in yourself, for you can achieve greatness beyond measure.

I hope our paths cross again someday, and you will share your incredible stories of success and fulfilment with me when they do. The world is waiting for your brilliance to shine, and I do not doubt that you will leave an indelible mark on its canvas.

Thank you for allowing me to be a part of your journey. I am honoured to have been your guide, and I have faith that you will go on to accomplish more than you can fathom. Believe in yourself, my friend, for the world, is yours to conquer.

I believe in you!

Chapter 10: Kik Alicha - The Heartwarming Comfort Food

"Things don't Turn Up until Somebody Turns Them Up." –
James A Garfield.

As I unveiled the chapters of my transformation, I aimed to ignite a spark within you. This book isn't your typical recipe-laden tome; it's a roadmap for self-discovery.

You might have noticed this book is void of the traditional healthy, low-calorie recipes you usually would find in books like these. Throughout these pages, I've emphasised one crucial point: there's no one-size-fits-all solution. Sure, I've sprinkled some ideas your way, but the path you choose, the goals you set and the foods you eat are uniquely yours to choose. It's about finding what resonates with you, and what fuels your journey.

There is one dish, though, I discovered on my journey that I'd like to share with you because it has helped me truly through some of my craving struggles along the way. I have hesitated to put in this book because it's essential for you to find your way, to find the dishes that work for you and fit your needs. But ultimately, depriving you of this recipe wouldn't have been right either.

As you can imagine, when you start lowering your calorie intake, you will soon find yourself fighting hunger pangs, but the real devil leading you into temptation is the cravings. Those miserable cravings that mess with your head, and you can't seem to shake them off.

I quickly learned that I needed to fill my stomach as early as possible in the morning to avoid the hunger pangs that always led to cravings. That has been quite a journey in itself. I started with the everyday things we usually have for breakfast, like porridge, but soon discovered that it just didn't get me through the day without getting sidetracked and taking in more food than I should.

I had a period that I would eat a bowl of cooked pasta in the morning, which again seemed to be fulfilling and even though I would feel full it somehow didn't stop my cravings.

For several months, I was feverishly searching and trying dishes that would be both fulfilling and not an invasion of my daily calorie goal. I tried various dishes, but somehow, they never seemed to help me through my hunger and craving periods.

Until the day I came across this Ethiopian dish, Kik Alicha, which has helped me through the toughest of times, it has been my go-to dish, the only one that never has let me down.

The story behind Kik Alicha is a tale of resourcefulness, creativity, and a deep connection to the land. Like many others in Ethiopian cuisine, this dish originates from the country's cultural tapestry. Ethiopia, known for its rich culinary heritage, has a long history of using locally sourced ingredients to create dishes that are not only delicious but also deeply nourishing.

Kik Alicha's name is derived from two key components: "Kik" signifies split yellow peas, the primary ingredient in the dish, while "Alicha" refers to the cooking method of slow stewing with fragrant spices. This preparation method embodies the heart and soul of Ethiopian cooking, where spices and herbs are lovingly combined to create layers of flavour.

Kik Alicha's roots can be traced back to the Ethiopian

Orthodox Christian fasting tradition, during which followers abstain from meat and dairy products. The need to create flavourful and satisfying vegetarian dishes led to the development of recipes like Kik Alicha, which continue to be enjoyed not only during fasting periods but throughout the year. I made this dish one evening as a dinner with some flatbread, and after I had entered my calories in my calorie counter, I was amazed at how low-calorie this dish was. The best revelation was that I still didn't feel hungry the following day, which was a novelty.

This made me wonder about this dish, so I did a trial and made myself one cup of Kik Alicha every morning to see how I would fare. That's when I learned I struck upon something that still, to this day I can't quite explain. After eating my portion of this dish, I would feel no hunger all day but the unexplainable was that I would have no cravings.

Initially, I thought this was just a fluke, so I introduced it to my daughter to try it out for a week. Same results. As she works in an office where her colleagues continuously talk about food, while they have the food channel on the big overhead screen, she was prone to feel hungry all day. During the week she had Kik Alicha in the morning, she felt no hunger nor cravings all day.

The preparation of Kik Alicha is a labour of love. It starts with split yellow peas, a nutritional powerhouse that is not only high in protein but also rich in essential vitamins and minerals. These peas are soaked, which helps reduce their cooking time and enhances their digestibility. I usually soak a good bunch overnight so I can prepare a week's worth of breakfast pots. After the soaking, I rinse the peas very well and then put them in a pot where I allow them to slowly simmer covered in water with a medley of spices, such as turmeric, cumin, and garlic for forty-five minutes. The result is a fragrant, aromatic stew with a velvety texture. Once cooked, I divide them into little pots that I pop into the microwave in the morning for two minutes, and I feel satisfied all day.

Kik Alicha is not only a flavourful delight but also a nutritional powerhouse. The yellow split peas are a fantastic source of plant-based protein, making Kik Alicha an excellent choice for vegetarians and vegans. A single serving of Kik Alicha can provide approximately 10-12 grams of protein, contributing to overall muscle health and satiety. The dish is also rich in dietary fibre, promoting healthy digestion and helping to maintain stable blood sugar levels. A serving of Kik Alicha can offer around 6-8 grams of dietary fibre. Yellow peas are also a source of essential vitamins and minerals, including folate, iron, and potassium. These nutrients support overall health and well-being.

Kik Alicha is naturally low in fat, making it a heart-healthy choice. My breakfast serving of Kik Alicha (about 1 cup) contains around 150-200 calories, varying based on portion size and the cooking method of course.

Kik Alicha has helped me with my weight loss and has helped me beat the hunger pangs and deceive cravings along the way. It has helped me feel full and satisfied, supporting my weight loss by reducing my overall calorie intake. As with any dietary choice, it's essential to consider your overall eating habits and calorie intake in the context of your weight loss goals of course.

THE END